Action Research
for Business,
Nonprofit,
& Public
Administration

Action Research
for Business, Nonprofit, & Public Administration

A Tool for Complex Times

E. Alana James
Jones International University, Walden University

Tracesea Slater
Colorado Technical University

Alan Bucknam
Notchcode Creative

Los Angeles | London | New Delhi
Singapore | Washington DC

Los Angeles | London | New Delhi
Singapore | Washington DC

FOR INFORMATION

SAGE Publications, Inc.
2455 Teller Road
Thousand Oaks, California 91320
E-mail: order@sagepub.com

SAGE Publications Ltd.
1 Oliver's Yard
55 City Road
London, EC1Y 1SP
United Kingdom

SAGE Publications India Pvt. Ltd.
B 1/I 1 Mohan Cooperative Industrial Area
Mathura Road, New Delhi 110 044
India

SAGE Publications Asia-Pacific Pte. Ltd.
33 Pekin Street #02-01
Far East Square
Singapore 048763

Acquisitions Editor: Lisa Cuevas Shaw
Editorial Assistant: Mayan White
Production Editor: Astrid Virding
Copy Editor: Pam Schroeder
Typesetter: Hurix Systems Pvt. Ltd.
Proofreader: Laura Webb
Indexer: William Ragsdale
Cover Designer: Anupama Krishnan
Marketing Manager: Helen Salmon
Permissions Editor: Karen Ehrmann

Copyright © 2012 by SAGE Publications, Inc.

Printed in the United States of America.

Library of Congress Cataloging-in-Publication Data

James, E. Alana.
Action research for business, nonprofit, and public administration : a tool for complex times / E. Alana James, Tracesea Slater, Alan Bucknam.
    p. cm.
Includes bibliographical references and index.
ISBN 978-1-4129-9164-3 (pbk.)

1. Action research. 2. Organizational learning. 3. Organizational change. I. Slater, Tracesea. II. Bucknam, Alan. III. Title.

H62.J344 2012
001.4--dc23   2011022879

This book is printed on acid-free paper.

11 12 13 14 15 10 9 8 7 6 5 4 3 2 1

Contents

Preface

This book is written for the graduate student who has struggled with bridging the theory of action research (AR) to the practice of how to complete a project. Having taught AR to students in business, nonprofit, and public administration for a doctorate of management program, we saw several challenges that they regularly faced:

- Becoming lost and wasting precious time, causing them to struggle at the end,

- Approaching AR as though it was another form of research, most usually qualitative,

- Missing the point of achieving measurable outcomes,

- Not delving deeply into reflection or reflexion and therefore learning nothing about their own culpability in the process,

- Accomplishing fantastic outcomes yet not bridging the gap to write them as research and, therefore, not getting their work published.

Quoting one of our students, "When I learn a new skill, I like a cookbook." This text answers that need, giving recipes for both basic and advanced practices. The purpose of this book is to guide graduate students in business, nonprofit, and public administration toward successful completion of research projects. We believe that, with that success, they will choose to use AR on an ongoing basis to make their personal and professional worlds mirror their vision.

First and foremost, this is written for either masters- or doctoral-level students in business, nonprofit, or public administration. The courses in which it should be adopted are those that range from beginning research to the specific use of AR in the field. Beginning researchers will find solid basic methodological writing that will help them make choices for class-level projects. Advanced students, or those choosing to use AR for dissertations will find the necessary citations and links to seminal literature that they need to ensure academic rigor. Having mentored doctoral students using AR, who were helpful in outlining elements missing from other texts, we feel confident that this book fills those gaps.

Because this book is meant to be a companion to theoretical texts such as Reason and Bradbury (2008), the major content area discussions within the field of AR are interwoven as the concepts impact practice. These include but are not limited to: reflection and reflexivity, complexity science, the logic of failure, emancipatory research potential, networked AR, and democracy as evident and pertaining to working in groups. Professors or instructors who may be new to teaching AR will find clear guidelines for proposal writing, informed consent documentation, graphic organizers to help

Action Research for Business, Nonprofit, and Public Administration

students manage their practice, and a protocol for weekly report writing to structure final analysis.

Our students stated that they needed both in-depth discussion and a ways and means to search the text easily when they needed to answer a question. To this end, you will find six chapters that address the different stages of writing an AR proposal (Chapter 2), beginning a project (Chapter 3), designing and obtaining measurements for ongoing actions (Chapter 4), working with people and groups (Chapter 5), doing AR in networked environments (Chapter 6), and finally, analyzing results and writing the final report (Chapter 7). The chapter subheadings are in the form of questions, allowing students to quickly find information when it is needed. All sections end with reflective questions aimed at helping students develop an ongoing reflective and reflexive practice. Every chapter ends with next steps and additional readings to help them dig deeper into the rich literature that surrounds this methodology. The book's design is approachable to all forms and levels of learning, including regular use of pictures, stories, pullouts, and illustrations to capture interest and foster understanding.

A textbook such as this is not a lone act. We need to acknowledge the input received from our reviewers. Because they plan to adopt the book in the courses they teach, the reviewers increased the specificity of small details that they suggested we include. This provided an immeasurable benefit when it came to fine-tuning, and it is with heartfelt thanks that we acknowledge:

Jan Arsenault, New England College

Edwin D. Bell, Winston Salem State University

Hilary Bradbury Huang, USC

Colleen Casey, University of Texas at Arlington

Paul L. Dann, New England College

Martha H. Ezzell, Ph.D., Carlow University

Jessica Heineman-Pieper, George Mason University

Elisabeth Hiles, Boston College

Melissa Houlett, College of Mount St. Joseph

Gherissi Labben Thouraya, École Hôtelière de Lausanne

Marco Tavanti, DePaul University

Introduction

Welcome to *Action Research for Business, Nonprofits, and Public Administration: A Tool for Complex Times.* This book is primarily a textbook for masters- and doctorate-level students, although we hope that you will find it so helpful that you will keep it on your bookshelf and continue to engage in the practice of AR long after you finish the course you are in. AR can become a way of life because of the power it offers us as practitioners. Working the steps and the cycles keeps several things that are very important to strategic planning and change management in the forefront of our brains. High among these are the requirement to continually delve into the literature of our fields, to take action steps while measuring their outcomes as we go, and finally to develop ourselves as reflective and reflexive practitioners.

A person has only to read the twitter streams searching for *action research* to get a taste of the confusion students often feel when faced with actually doing the process. Our own students are equally confused after a semester of AR theory. It is for this reason that we wrote this book, aimed at helping you, the student practitioner, easily maneuver through three cycles and processes required of you as you complete what may be your first graduate-level research project.

After reading Chapters 1 through 3 of this book, we hear statements like the following:

> Why didn't we have this book last quarter? It would have made AR understandable and clear!

> This really put into perspective what AR is and how it can be applied.

> I like the clarity and simplicity of the writing. Very focused and on target for the reader.

As one of our students commented, "When I learn a new skill, I like a cookbook." While perhaps more than a cookbook, we hope that we have kept true to the purpose of helping you directly complete the work while not getting caught in our own love of the process and its intricacies too much. Because we want this to be a book that lives on a bookshelf in your business, nonprofit, or public administration office long after you finish this course, we have also included Chapters 5, 6, and 8, which should also be useful to your continuing process as a leader in your work environment.

Professors and others who are well versed in AR literature will notice that the way we describe the process is atypical from the four-step cycle commonly referred to. The change to a measurable action step is to help you get over two hurdles where we saw many students break down. In the old four-part discussion, you might have been tempted to either measure every possible thing about your current situation but never stray into taking actionable steps toward positive change. Equally probable would be the reverse, where you might take lots of positive moving forward actions but not capture them adequately with data. It is our hope that our three-part cycle of discovery, measurable action, and reflection—where discovery is used for a review of literature, measurable action is where you get the work done and collect your data, and reflection where you capture your reflective and reflexive data—will keep your project both moving forward and in line with standard research practices, allowing your work to be more easily published.

This book is intended therefore, to be practical, straightforward, and full of examples. It is written in a style that allows you to both read it cover to cover or dive in and out of it as your process requires. The book is formatted with wide margins, lots of pictures, easy callouts of important information, and so on to meet the demands of busy businesspeople in the 21st century. We did not include an extensive conversation about any of the particular theoretical issues that are widely discussed within the AR community. We hope, however, that we include enough citations and references to those conversations that you can easily follow an interest area to the source material.

A quick road map through this book will show you that Chapters 1, 2, and 3 should give you a firm basis of understanding and the ability to both design and begin to implement an AR project. Chapter 4 helps you understand how you might marry AR to basic qualitative, quantitative, and mixed methods design as you go forward in your project with some measurable actions. Chapter 5 discusses the skills and issues inherent in working as part of a participatory group or with other people in general. Chapter 6 goes into the specifics needed to employ AR over a large area, as part of a network, or in some other extended environment. Chapter 7 takes you through a basic analysis and helps you write a solid final report, depending upon the needs of your stakeholders. The last chapter contains final comments from other professors around the world, our own students, and ourselves. Finally, we include four appendices with practical tools aimed to help establish good practices from the beginning. Included are: a sample outline for an AR proposal, the protocol we use for weekly AR reflections, the layout for an AR table of measurable actions, and a facilitation guide for those wanting to implement a large-scale networked participatory action research project (NPAR).

We close this introduction with a post taken from the SAGE action research blog (http://arj-journal.blogspot.com/2011/01/dear-action-research-melissa-nylander.html). We believe Melissa captures much of the heart and soul of AR and why we love this process. We hope that, at the end of your foray into this methodological environment, you do too. Also please visit our site at www.ar4everything.com where you will find additional and ancillary materials for this book.

Sincerely, your authors,

E. Alana, Tracesea, and Alan

Action Research for Business, Nonprofit, and Public Administration

Dear Action Research,

I have a confession: I can't get you off my mind.

I first learned about you, Action Research, a year ago through a fellow graduate student. She pointed you out to me on the course register, and I was immediately smitten. But, circumstances being what they were, I wasn't able to pursue you. So I waited, pining from afar, never allowing myself to entertain the thought of us being together. In the meantime, I tried to see other research methodologies. Some of them briefly held my interest, but they always turned out to be cold and aloof. Several of them even warned me about you. "Don't waste your time with Action Research," they said. "People will laugh at you," they said. And I believed them.

But never fully. When the opportunity arose, I signed up for a class that would allow me to get to know you better. I won't lie. My guard was up. At this point, I had heard so many contradicting things about you that my initial infatuation had become tarnished by wariness. You were so hard to pin down at first. The professor and my fellow students were constantly defining you by what you aren't rather than by what you are. Not empirical. Not generalizable. Not objective. I began to wonder if I'd ever be able to see you for who you truly are.

Gradually, you began to come into focus, and the skepticism I had carried with me into our relationship faded. I couldn't help but let our interactions get personal, which went against every prior experience I had ever had with research. In the past, when I had allowed myself to be human with respect to my research, other methodologies had rejected me outright. One even dumped me on the spot, saying that my honesty was not just unprofessional but unethical. The experience broke me.

But, Action Research, you accepted me. I know it sounds corny, but I'd never met a methodology like you before. Your willingness to see people (both subjects and researchers alike) as complex and dynamic beings has given me hope. I admire your ability to adapt to every situation without losing sight of your values.

Yet, there are still moments when I feel alienated from you. Action Research, you remain wrapped up in this swath of intellectual elitism, perhaps because you know that, if you step too far from the ivory tower, you'll have to work that much harder to prove yourself. So long as you have your publications and legions of well-educated followers, like the other research methodologies you must stand amongst, you will be safe. But, if you're really striving for justice, understanding, and a revolution in how we produce and disseminate knowledge, then put aside your insecurities. Do the soul searching you've asked me to do, and you may find that academia is your birthplace but perhaps not where you were meant to end up.

I hope things work out between us. Sometimes, after we've spent time together, I'm left with this euphoric feeling that I can barely contain. I get butterflies, and for a moment, I believe that all my naive, idealistic ambitions really can be realized. But then, I begin to wonder. Is this just a crush? Just some fleeting infatuation that will eventually crumble under the unbearable disappointment that descends when I realize that something I thought I loved was too good to be true?

Yours for now,

Melissa Nylander

Chapter 1.
Introducing the Three Steps of Action Research: A Tool for Complex Times and Situations

Action research (**AR**) and its counterpart, **participatory action research (PAR),** are powerful tools for people in business, nonprofits, and public administration who seek to create change in complex situations for the sake of sustainable improvement. In this chapter, we introduce the process, discuss why it is important, and explain how you might use it and what strategies you can employ to ensure your success.

We write this book making a few assumptions about you, our reader: Probably you are or have recently been in graduate school. You are an early to midcareer professional in business, nonprofit, or public administration. You are more than likely taking a class that requires this book, but it may be that you saw it on the bookshelf or while surfing a bookseller's website and decided to purchase it. You may be intending to work as a lone researcher (with support from the outside such as faculty and other students) or with a team (PAR) as you complete the AR process, and throughout, we will discuss both options.

Because AR and PAR solve complex problems and complexity describes much of our world, it makes sense that we have seen a rise in its use. Similar in

I believe quite simply that the small company of the future will be as much a research organization as it is a manufacturing company.
—*Edwin Herbert Land*

many ways to strategic planning, this process should seem familiar, yet many planning sessions often do not end with solid results measured over time. When we add the rigor of research, it becomes powerful. There are two reasons for this:

1. It transforms you, the researcher, as you grow in understanding of the issue(s) you study (Cunliffe, 2004, 2005; James, 2005, 2006a, 2009; Schön, 1983, 1987).

2. Data-driven decisions have increased power to influence stakeholders, and AR Research protocols insist that you gather data.

This chapter will address several questions:

- What is AR, and where did it come from?

- What are other methodologies that are similar to AR?

- What are the steps in the AR process?

- How does AR **methodology** use quantitative, qualitative, and mixed methods?

- Why is AR a methodology for complex times?

- How can I ensure success? Study failure!

We end each section with questions designed to help you drill deeper into the concepts in the reading, using this question mark to signal your reflection.

Reflective Questions

- ✦ What strategic planning efforts have you been involved with?
- ✦ What were the outcomes of those plans?

What Is Action Research, and Where Did It Come From?

AR is, in the most basic sense, a type of research that creates and measures change in a cyclical manner with the intention of overall positive growth throughout the process. This type of research is generally conducted in a collaborative manner by an individual person or team of people who are interested not only in studying a particular problem but also in creating solutions. When a team-based approach is used, this is generally referred to as PAR, and the stakeholders involved all share equally in the democratic research process. Although some collaboration is needed in all AR projects, a single researcher can go through the research process alone if chosen. Either approach has the aim of supporting actions that lead to satisfactory results for all those involved. Researchers and stakeholders define a problem, collect relevant information about the problem, take action, measure it using various research methods, and finally interpret the results. These steps, which are discussed in more detail later in this chapter and throughout the book, are continuously repeated to create the AR process. The desired end result of AR is always focused on positive change and solutions to benefit all those involved.

The history of AR and its ultimate origins are often debated in the literature; however, most agree that Kurt Lewin was one of the founding fathers of this research methodology. Lewin, a social psychologist, fled Nazi Germany for the United States during World War II. He went on to conduct various research projects, which were all aimed at creating some sort of social

If you want truly to understand something, try to change it.
—Kurt Lewin

change. Lewin's research was different from typical social research because it went against the idea of the researcher as an objective outsider who merely observes and records. His vision included the active participation of the researcher with the aim of achieving a particular goal. Lewin also believed in the inclusion of a variety of everyday people as practitioners, and his research was conducted in real-life situations. However, as noted by Greenwood and Levin (2007), Lewin's original view of AR as a short-term intervention was limiting, and eventually the focus of AR moved toward a more continuous and long-term process. In spite of this change, Lewin's work is commonly referred to as the basis of modern AR.

Bradbury, Mirvis, Neilsen, and Pamore (2008) continue this discussion of Lewin's early work with his students in manufacturing. They point out that, in 1948, Coch and French showed that participation in AR experiments proved to be a "unique means to reduce resistance to change" (in Reason & Bradbury, 2008, p. 78). In times of frequent and often dramatic change (such as the kind faced around the world today), AR has proven itself time and again to help alleviate the stress by engaging the mind in discovery of new ideas, data gathering about actions taken, and reflecting by the practitioners involved.

What Are Other Methodologies That Are Similar to Action Research?

Academia is not known for its easy adoption of new ideas. Thus, AR, **action science (AS),** and all their participatory *cousins* (variations or similar methodologies built on similar premises) were born over the last 50 years and more and have struggled to prove their legitimacy. During this time, different champions rose to defend action in research (Reason & Bradbury, 2008). Many of these saw what they did as distinct and called it by a different name. We will discuss several of the well-known and emerging AR cousins: AS, PAR, community-based participatory research (CBPR), action learning (AL), appreciative inquiry (AI), living theory, and participatory action leadership action research (PALAR). They follow similar processes for work, but each has a slightly different outlook. Remember, this is not intended to offer enough detail for you as a researcher to use only these materials on which to build the theoretical base for your work. If one resonates with you, you will want to use part of your discovery time looking into it. As with all cousins, there are similarities and differences in outlook, specifics of the cyclic nature of the methodology, and philosophical direction for each.

Action Science

The work of Chris Argyris (1990, 2002a, 2002b) is closely linked to AS in the organizational development world. His best-known work may be that on defensiveness in organizations, and thus AS is aimed at helping an organization grow past toxic behaviors. AS is currently supported by an active network on http://www.actionscience.com/ (Network, 2011), which states:

> Action science is a strategy for designing situations that foster effective stewardship of any type of organization. It is a framework for learning how to be more effective in

A student wanted to bring change to the way the union and management in his organization dealt with personal family leave. He used AR to learn more about the options, discuss the issues with key personnel, and propose options. The final outcome at the end of a 10-week class was that the stakeholders were meeting to discuss the issues.

groups. It aims to help individuals, groups, and organizations to develop a readiness and ability to change to meet the needs of an often changing environment.

To help individuals in groups to learn how to overcome barriers to organizational change, action science does not simply focus on improving the participants' problem-solving or decision-making skills. It also does not look only at making incremental changes (e.g., identifying opportunities; finding, correcting, reducing, or eliminating threats) in the external environment. Without eschewing these concerns, action science focuses on looking inward, learning new frameworks, and establishing new routines.

Friedman and Rogers (2008) conceptualize the process in the following way. First, using a community of inquiry (a community of practice focused on using the scientific practices of building theory and then testing them), they develop theories of action. These are causal theories about why we do the things we do, and in them, we make assumptions that our behavior is driven at least to some extent by our ideals. Frames are designed that elaborate on the logic or make sense of the circumstances we are studying—then we test the frame. In other words, by objectifying the ideas, actions and drives into a hypothetical frame, we can "balance advocacy with inquiry" (p. 255). *Advocacy* is defined as advancing our ideas about the situation, and inquiry is our test of those ideas.

Because AS has been used actively as a methodology for more than 50 years, it too has developed cousins

Action Research for Business, Nonprofit, and Public Administration

or offshoots. Key in these are action design, learning pathways, debriefing with good judgment, and learning from success. Two other major streams of actionable theories have their bases in AS. Argyris (1990, 2002a, 2002b), as an example, developed deep understanding on the ways and means in which defensiveness plays into our frames of behavior.

In the field of organizational development, **sensemaking** has grown in recent years to encompass and expand upon many of these ideas, with the work of Weick (1969, 1979, 1995, 2001, 2009) standing out. Similar to working with frames, "sensemaking involves the ongoing retrospective development of plausible images that rationalize what people are doing" (Weick, Sutcliffe, & Obstfeld, 2005). Beyond Weick's writing, you will find additional readings included at the end of each chapter. Several are examples of similar issues as AR practitioners work with knowledge development in organizations.

Participatory Action Research

PAR brings the power of diverse voices to bear on the issue under study and will be discussed throughout this book because AR often branches into PAR issues that are suited to group or team exploration or where the voice of all stakeholders is needed in a more democratizing, egalitarian format. PAR has within its structure the likelihood of transformation and emancipation as researchers and participatory partners question reality as currently experienced with an eye on how to improve it. These elements arise in business, nonprofit, or public administration

Knowledge is always gained through action and for action. From this starting point, to question the validity of social knowledge is to question, not how to develop a reflective science about action, but how to develop genuinely well-informed action—how to conduct an action science.
—Bill Torbert

as researchers work in cross-cultural or international teams, confronting the differences of viewpoints among participants.

Herr and Anderson (2005) point out that the philosophical belief in development through inclusion of people who normally would be seen as being served (the clients, the lower classes, or the customers, depending on your context) rather than as managers, designers, or researchers was largely galvanized in the United States by the work of Paolo Friere. In his *Pedagogy of the Oppressed,* Friere (2000) developed the theme of individuals becoming truly human through their inquiry and cooperation to pursue the best in life and for their worlds.

Participatory work revolutionized research starting in the 1970s (Herr & Anderson, 2005). However it is employed, facilitating PAR means that you, as researcher, are one voice among equals in the team that conducts the research. You may come up against or struggle with issues of community empowerment, policy change, or the development of sustainable assets or capacities. All are issues about which strong opinions emerge.

During the 1980s and 1990s, the federal grant structure for nonprofits working with at-risk populations and the disabled insisted that the voices in collaborative work include a democratic representation of the stakeholders, including clients. For your study, you will have to decide the depth and practicality of how you will engage your constituents or clients, how much time your project can devote to gathering desperate voices, and how you will report your **findings** so that others may have access to disagree.

Challenges within PAR are that, strictly speaking, all voices need to agree on the analysis and results at the end of the project and have consensus on what will be published or how. For any researcher wanting to include diverse points of view and work as a group, but for whom publishing considerations may need to held in abeyance, we suggest calling it AR and having an advisory team of diverse voices with whom you interact as with equals.

Community-Based Participatory Research

Starting in the 1970s, practitioners in education, health care, and public administration began to question when and to what extent they should involve the people who would be subject to the ideas of research in the research process.

Used primarily to address disparities between research and action in health, welfare, and environmental issues, **community-based participatory research (CBPR)** brings community stakeholders into the discussion of how to reach constituents with healthful messages and to help change their behavior. As a participatory research, CBPR is a very close cousin to PAR, with groups of citizens acting as equal partners with research scientists. This builds on the model within public administration for citizens to be asked to sit in on panels or review boards and take a full step further. With CBPR, they become active researchers with equal rights with the rest of the team. Widely sponsored by various National Institutes of Health initiatives, in a recent report on CBPR, they say:

> CBPR is a collaborative research approach that is designed to ensure and establish structures for participation by communities affected by the issue being studied, representatives of organizations, and researchers in all aspects of the research process to improve health and well-being through taking action, including social change. The goal is improving health and well-being of members of the community, however defined for a given research project, by means of taking actions that bring about intended change and minimize negative consequences of such change. (Viswanathan, et al., 2004)

Hughes (2008) adds to the discussion of AR in health care, which is not exclusively CBPR, by pointing out things that are, in our view, similar to when and how we adopt AR in any circumstance. He lists six reasons that people would adopt one of these methodologies:

- belief that employment of the methodology will be helpful

- the requirement that research tie to past literature or research

- increased levels of communication and knowledge about your organization

- time required to share ideas and opinions with your peers and perhaps your clients

Action Research for Business, Nonprofit, and Public Administration

- the development of data on which to base future plans

- growth in economic efficiencies

He goes on to discuss the relevance for these methods in complex situations, such as health care (but we would expand this discussion to any organizational arena and education). Because complexity science has taught us to look at large numbers of autonomous agents or situations, each adapting to stimuli in their personal contexts, yet who play off of each other as part of the greater system, practitioners require methodology that is likewise flexible in order to capture overarching patterns as well as specifics. Hughes makes a good case that it is the insider nature of most AR (see more in Chapter 2) that allows a greater potential for understanding both the wider organizational patterns and the specific contexts that drive complex change.

Action Learning

Action learning (AL) sits somewhere in the middle of the theoretical spectrum between AR and AI, although others would argue with us that this analogy is soft and that the continuum of philosophies that drive these methodological ideas is not straightforward. Still, we mention it here due to its historical significance as a link between individual and organizational learning, particularly relevant in today's world of "learning organizations." Since the advent of postmodernistic ideas and critical theories, AL has grown in its push to critically analyze the learning within a situation through the use of protocols that enhance inquiry (Pedler & Burgoyne, 2008).

This call for critical analysis will be addressed again in Chapter 8 as we develop a call to action for those working with these methodologies.

There is a variety of AL: **action learning action research (ALAR)**. An interesting format, researchers manage the project while they study it (Coghlan & Coughlan, 2006; Greenwood & Levin, 2007).

Appreciative Inquiry

Developed by David Cooperrider and Sursh Srivastva in the 1980s, **appreciative inquiry** is based on the idea that whatever you measure will grow; therefore, if you want an organization to grow in a positive light, you should measure what is already positive and set up actions to increase those things. Cooperrider and Whitney (2005) say:

> Appreciative Inquiry is about the co-evolutionary search for the best in people, their organizations, and the relevant world around them. In its broadest focus, it involves systematic discovery of what gives "life" to a living system when it is most alive, most effective, and most constructively capable in economic, ecological, and human terms. AI involves, in a central way, the art and practice of asking questions that strengthen a system's capacity to apprehend, anticipate, and heighten positive potential. It centrally involves the mobilization of inquiry through the crafting of the "unconditional positive question" often involving hundreds or sometimes thousands of people.

AI is systematized into the five Ds: define, discover, dream, design, destiny. In the definition stage,

A student wanted to look into stress in the workplace and determine what could be done at his company. The discovery section led him to the ethical issues of treating people as objects. He measured the similarities between responses to his survey in the United States and abroad and concluded that these issues are international in scope.

people come to an awareness that change is needed, then during discovery, they talk about when the organization is at its best. The dream section is similar to brainstorming in a strategic planning session, with everyone envisioning the best for the organization. Design teams are then empowered to help bring back practical steps to achieve those dreams, and finally, in the destiny step, those designs are placed in action.

In Reason and Bradbury (2008), Zandee and Cooperrider (2008) overview their two decades of AI work by pointing out these benefits to an AI approach, saying it "illuminates the miracle of life . . . questions attributes taken for granted . . . envisions new potential . . . creates knowledge embedded in relationships . . . and enables just and sustainable co-existence" (pp. 193–195). Ludema and Fry (2008) go on to say it has created a "positive revolution in change" (p. 281).

Living Theory

Living theory is a theoretical construct of Jack Whitehead and Jean McNiff (2006), and all their students and people they have worked with over the years. It suggests that the highest form of our work is toward our ideals and that AR practice, run in an infinite number of cycles and throughout our lifetimes, increases our natural transformation into practitioners who live those ideals. Living theory is primarily applied to educational practice, but we feel that people involved in business, non-profits, and public administration will benefit from these ideas as well.

I do not separate my scientific inquiry from my life. For me it is really a quest for life, to understand life and to create what I call living knowledge—knowledge which is valid for the people with whom I work and for myself.
—*Marja-Liisa Swantz*

Reflective Questions

✦ Can you see both the similarities and differences across the variety of AR and its close counterparts?

✦ Given the issue you want to face and on which you wish to develop positive change, is there any one particular type of AR that you might want to look into more?

Participatory Action Learning and Action Research

Being developed by Ortun Zuber-Skerritt (2011), who is perhaps best known for her work on AR as professional development, PALAR merges the "importance of self-directed learning and development to the very diverse constituencies in the fields of action research, and leadership and organization development." PALAR emphasizes new integrated concepts of AL, PAR, and the basic tenets of AR. With its discussion focused on leadership, PALAR is

> actively creative, innovative, collaborative, shared and self-developed in partnership with others. It involves taking responsibility for, not control over, people through networking, and orchestrating human energy towards a holistic vision and an outcome that best serves the common interest. A good PALAR process is one in which action leadership can emerge from anywhere in the group; and leaders and followers are often changing places if all are to learn. Action leaders are passionate; they inspire, and help an idea to cascade to other people like a spark taking flame, as depicted in the ancient Chinese saying that launches this chapter: "A single spark can start a prairie fire." (Zuber-Skerritt, 2011, 7)

What Are the Steps in the Action Research Process?

We anticipate that upper most in your mind right now is, "What will I be doing?"

It all starts with a question you want to answer that relates to a problem you want to solve. This problem may develop in any number of ways from your environment. For instance, you may have clients or constituents who need answers, a new law may create new requirements for the way you do business, budget cuts may be affecting your operation or staff morale, and the future may seem uncertain. Whether in business, nonprofit organizations, or public administration offices, what we do is influenced by the greater context in which we work.

This is what makes AR significantly different from other forms of research. In most methodologies, you start with a question you want to answer—here, you have questions, but your burning desire is to make a difference to the situation as well as measure it. Because our ideas of what we want to accomplish are also determined by our individual contexts and worldviews, AR forces us to be inclusive of other ways of thinking and acting through its requirement on an initial discovery process. Finally, you will discover that the actions you take evolve quickly because of AR's requirement to measure outcomes and adjust during the process.

Throughout this book, you will find that we assist you through highlighting examples of student work in action. For the purpose of this early section, we will use the story of one of our students. He managed small, rural health clinics and was concerned about increasing the level of safety compliance.

The diagram in Figure 1.1 draws out the three steps he took. AR developed with the conceptualization of the process in four steps. Over years of facilitating

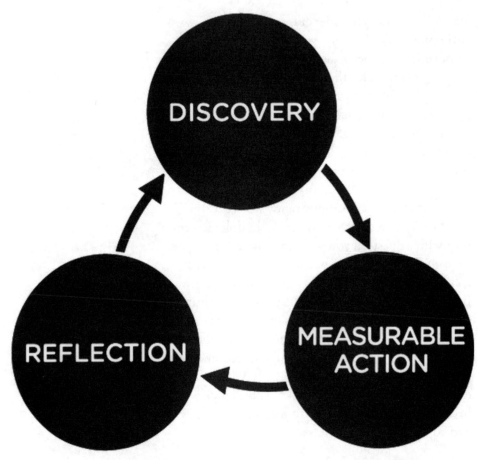

Alan Bucknam | Notchcode | 2011

Figure 1.1

the process, it became clear to us that people broke down in two major ways: Either they never moved from data gathering (took no real actions), or they did not adequately measure the actions they did take. For this reason, we reformatted the steps, merging two of them into what we now call *measurable action*. As shown in Figure 1.1, we suggest you conceptualize AR cycles in three steps:

Action Research for Business, Nonprofit, and Public Administration

Discovery

First, you have to discover what is true now then investigate what others have done about the problem you wish to improve when in similar circumstances. For instance, you might look into data your company has collected, or you might search on the web or talk with colleagues in different parts of the world looking for success stories about people who completed the changes you are seeking.

Our student was involved with a team using PAR. In their discovery process, they did three things:

a. They investigated the areas in which they fell short of the standards for safety (this required looking at what we call archival data—back reports from safety officials).

b. They researched on the web how others had been successful in turning the same issues around in their practices.

c. They diligently watched what was going on to be able to better classify where the real problems lay.

They asked themselves who was more responsible: new hires who might not understand the procedures or older employees who might have fallen into lazy habits, or perhaps a mixture.

From discovery, you (with AR) or your team (with PAR) will go on to decide what steps you might take toward your goal. You will also have to discover what research methodologies and methods you can use to measure the outcomes of those actions—this is Step 2.

Somewhere, something incredible is waiting to be known.
—Carl Sagan

Measurable Action

This step has evolved in our teaching from two (first action then measurement) to one. When conceptualized as measurable action, we find beginning researchers are less inclined to run right into taking an action step without seriously considering how they will measure the outcomes of their actions. Evaluation techniques have a lot to teach us here as they insist that we first gather baseline data from which we can measure change. We will say more about the links between evaluation and measurement in Chapter 3.

In our example from the rural health agency, the PAR team found that, rather than a human resource issue as they thought, it appeared that people were most likely to forget the use of sterile latex gloves in certain areas of the clinic, thus diminishing their procedure versus use-of-glove ratio. They decided to see if the use of signs to remind people of the need for safety would help.

First, they had to establish baseline data. This resulted in their asking everyone to log their activities in the room (giving them the number of activities), and from that data, they could compare the number of tests being run versus the number of used gloves. The result was X. Would putting up signs help everyone remember to wear gloves? They continued to monitor the use of the room against the number of gloves—things improved, but did not reach 100%.

In their next team meeting, they convened with their data to reflect on their first cycle of research.

Reflection

This is the third step. It is said that the importance of being a reflective practitioner in any field makes

A student manager in a fire department looked into how to improve morale and efficiency within his department. Using PAR, he discovered that some shifts had lower morale than others, thus allowing him to isolate conditions. A major outcome included increased team solidarity and plans to implement future trainings.

the difference between evolving to become an expert or staying as a moderately good practitioner. Involved in the reflection step in AR is an implied willingness to delve deeply into both what is working and what is not working in your research process.

Our rural health team looked at the data and saw improvement but not as much as they would have liked. They needed everyone to participate 100% in safety standards. It was not a failure; they did not need to start over, but they did need to build on this success. In their reflection, they noticed that the signs had also impacted employee attitudes, calling attention to their focus on the health and safety of everyone. They asked themselves how they could build on this beginning. That led them into their next discovery cycle, but we will leave them there for now.

A full discussion of these steps, with examples of success and failures within each, is in Chapter 3.

Reflective Question

+ What questions do you have about the specifics of the AR cycle that remain unanswered?

How Does Action Research Methodology Use Quantitative, Qualitative, and Mixed Methods?

Merriam-Webster defines *methodology* as "a particular procedure or set of procedures," while the same source defines *methods* as "a systematic procedure or mode of inquiry or a systematic plan." AR is a methodology, a set of procedures, and we typically use qualitative and quantitative methods to measure the results of our actions. As businesspeople, nonprofit managers, or public servants, we might be able to employ AR with less-than-rigorous measurement or methods. However, once we step into the academic world, we need to also meet those standards.

Chapter 4 examines methodologies in more depth, but as we have found that beginning student researchers often get lost in the terminology, a little overview is appropriate here. Building upon the definitions of *Merriam-Webster,* AR as a methodology gives you both the process of your work and its theoretical basis as research. This strength comes from its history, the thousands of researchers who have preceded you, and the academic rigor to which AR has been subjected, to stand out as a methodology that can be considered viable. You need to understand AR well enough to discuss it in the methodology section of your proposal and your final paper. You need to understand its process (the three steps as we employ them) and how each step relates to your work.

Let's start with how you reason issues through. We induce (use inductive reasoning or logic) to construct an idea out of parts. AR is inductive, and this means that we use qualitative data collection methods most of the time, but not exclusively. Inductive reasoning allows us to deepen our understanding of our lived experience, apply the expanded view to new contexts, and study the results, always building on our base of knowledge as we grow. Deductive reasoning attempts to show that a conclusion follows (is sound) from a set of hypotheses. Quantitative methods are used here.

> **Follow effective action with quiet reflection. From the quiet reflection will come even more effective action.**
> —*Peter F. Drucker*

Deductive studies ask that if something is true, than can we also not deduce these other factors to be true also? Many AR studies have reasons to employ both types of reasoning.

You will employ either qualitative, quantitative, or mixed methods as you measure the distance from your baseline toward your desired outcome. Qualitative methods ask people questions and elicit data from them in the form of words. Quantitative methods ask questions that are translated into numbers, and those numbers are analyzed using statistical means. Mixed methods use the qualitative and quantitative to reinforce or repudiate data collected perhaps over a period of time. Generally, qualitative methods are good for small populations as you gain a lot of information from a few people and can drill deep into the human factors in the subject you are studying. Quantitative methods are needed when studying a large population across a specific range of variables. On a practical level, qualitative research is easier to implement but takes a long time to analyze. Quantitative research takes longer to specifically design and test the instrument, but once the data is collected, it can be organized and analyzed using statistical tools and software in a relatively short time. To do mixed methods well, you need to understand the challenges of both methods and what it takes to overcome these concerns.

AR and PAR are usually concerned with organizational development, community empowerment, or issues of policy change, but in your role as the

It takes a trained and discerning researcher to keep the goal in sight, and to detect evidence of the creeping progress toward it.
—John C. Polanyi

Table 1.1

	Action Research	Participatory Action Research	Pure Knowledge Research
Role of Researcher	Project manager—Learning and implementing new ideas or solutions	Equal part of a group that is studying and improving practice	In charge—collecting and analyzing data.
Application	Development of new solutions to issues, professional development	Developing, applying, and testing new processes, procedures, or contextual relationships	Developing new knowledge

Reflective Questions

✦ You may find yourself naturally drawn to gathering data in one or another particular manner—do your ideas fit the general discussion of when you might use either qualitative or quantitative methods as described above?

researcher, the specifics of the application may be different and are decidedly different within your role when conducting standard research. Because these intricacies can seem somewhat confusing, we offer Table 1.1.

Creswell (2009) reminds us that the methods we choose all are intricately dependent upon the **purpose** of our research. Because AR's purpose is to make a difference in some aspect of life, as a researcher, you would ordinarily include qualitative methods. At the same time, there may be the need to double check or triangulate what you think you learned from interviews or focus groups by checking with the wider population. In this case, you may decide to develop the survey and ask a broader population of people to either verify or dispute their initial understanding.

Chapter 4 reviews the methods we have seen student researchers employ most often, the basics of

Action Research for Business, Nonprofit, and Public Administration

qualitative coding, as well as a few common issues and practices with quantitative methods.

Why Is Action Research a Methodology for Complex Times?

The last two decades have seen an increase in people's understanding of complexity. Coming from the Latin word *complexus*, or entwined, complexity is much like threads in a Celtic knot, where by looking, it becomes difficult if not impossible to say where one stops and another begins. In a scientific sense, it may be defined as properties that make a situation or set of relationships difficult to discuss accurately, even when given almost complete information about its component parts and their interrelatedness.

This greater understanding of how many realms in our lives are complex has led to significant impacts for both research and strategic outcomes. Much research is conducted in laboratories because they can limit the number of variables impacting the outcomes of their studies. Life comes with unlimited variables and therefore is complex, especially when we choose to vary some aspect of it in order to build sustainable, long-term change. We argue that AR is perfect for practitioners making these types of changes (and data from around the world backs us up) because it sets a holding environment through which to manage change. *Holding environment* is the phrase used by Heifetz (2000) to address the fact that formal leaders in authority need to set a space where others can do their work, relieving some of the entwined aspects of

> **[We] become reflective researchers in situations of uncertainty, instability, uniqueness, and conflict.**
> *—Donald Schön*

the work to allow for focus on the issue, or the complex issues become daunting. Our previous research (James, 2005, 2006a) has shown that AR and PAR create just such a holding environment.

Was the rural health team facing a complex problem? Were a number of situations and motivations entwined to create what might look like a simple problem of people not reacting properly to health and safety regulations? How many reasons would people have for avoiding the proper use of gloves in the clinic? What influence did the working relationships within the office, the budget for materials, the management practices, and so on, have on this issue? Perhaps the employees:

- Had not received training.

- Were tired and forgetful.

- Did not eat lunch and were thinking more about being hungry (or any other complaint) than about safety.

- Conveyed the attitude that health and safety regulations did not matter.

- Were upset by budget cuts, and low morale influenced them to cut corners at work.

- Were out of gloves and chose not to go get more (perhaps they needed test results in a hurry).

- Were engaged in conversations that took their attention away from safety.

Each of these problems would have a different potential solution. We hope that this demonstrates how even a seemingly simple question may have complex issues that need to be faced before it is solved. We will tease out issues of complexity throughout the book.

Complex situations cause people to shut down as they are afraid of the difficulties of facing them. Say you wanted to solve world hunger, where would you start? How convinced would you be of your ability to create meaningful change? Similarly (and to use problems we have seen students tackle), employees faced with budget crises, risk management directors trying to stop unsafe practices, program managers trying to bring success to inner-city kids, public administration offices working to improve policy on human trafficking or human resource issues, people interested in making a workplace more friendly to diverse populations, or doctoral students trying to decide on their dissertation topics, all are complex problems. It follows then that part of why this methodology is important is the very human reason that it makes us feel more secure when we tackle the seemingly impossible task of change in complex situations.

How Can I Ensure Success? Study Failure!

Success means that you have achieved the goals or outcomes you set for your project. Depending on your context, these may range from a definite organizational change to a smaller beginning

Reflective Questions

✦ What situation are you considering for this research, and what positive change would you hope to make?

✦ Can you list the ways in which complexities may influence working on this issue?

implementation of a new process or perhaps answering a question about procedures. Before we talk about success, we should know a little about failure. Two sources of failure spring to mind: power issues within the organization (discussed in Chapter 5) or people who don't want to or are unable to change. Argyris (2002a) discusses people who don't change in terms of defensive reasoning and *the doom loop*. The high expectations people have of themselves and their fear and lack of understanding about failure lead them to react defensively when challenged by change. These reactions are characterized by lack of data, vague responses, and general avoidance. The way out, as Argyris saw it, was through reflexive double loop learning—in other words, we need to be trained in new reasoning skills, ones that objectively look at data and reflect on it to derive meaning. This is very similar to the AR process.

The topic of failure and how we avoid it or learn from it are threads throughout this book. Because of the multiple cycles in AR and its reflective portion, we hope to find the failures early and correct them.

Dietrich Dorner's (1996) work in cognitive behavior involved teams of people working with planning games (computer simulations) in the 1980s. His subjects included economists, managers, and designers who worked in a simulated environment where they manage the fate of a South African tribe. The tribe had a finite number of people, water, crops, and cattle. Their purpose was to increase the quality of life for the people. What consistently happened instead was that entire tribes died out. Dorner's work shows us the common threads of rational thought that consistently lead to failure. He points out that "failure does not strike like a bolt from the blue; it develops gradually according to its own logic" (p. 10).

We introduce failure in this chapter with a short discussion on a few of Dorner's findings and how AR and PAR help individuals overcome their likelihood due to the requirements of each step in the process.

1. Dorner's teams suffered from "failure to anticipate side effects and long-term repercussions" (p. 15). AR's cycle-by-cycle review of what is transpiring in a long-term process makes this far less likely. PAR makes use of a team structure, where many people can address the potential of each action long term. For instance, with the rural health example, a team member pointed out studies indicating that the effectiveness of signage is relatively short term. The signs become part of the background and are forgotten.

2. "The participants established their modus operandi in the first few sessions and did not alter it much later" (p .17). Because AR is a multicycle research process, there is continuous readjustment. The forced reflective cycle encourages the consideration of changes to heighten results.

A student investigated best practices for minority business leaders in an economic downturn. She developed a measurement tool and began to survey businesses as to how they adapt and survive. The results were inspirational to her entire PAR team, surviving to help them keep a positive outlook.

Reflective Questions

✦ Think about situations you were involved in or know of where outcomes were less than expected—do aspects of them fit Dorner's findings?

✦ What steps does Dorner's work suggest in order for you to ensure the success of your AR?

3. "Helplessness generates cynicism" (p. 18) with the implication here that decisions made from a cynical point of view tend to be reactionary rather than growth producing. AR is an inherently optimistic research methodology based on belief in creating and measuring positive change.

4. Finally and perhaps most importantly, Dorner found that failure stems from, "over involvement in projects which blind line managers to the emerging needs and changes within the situation" (p. 18). Because PAR requires consistent focus on the issue at hand, the tendency to be distracted by other things within the organization is lessened. This is part of the holding environment that was discussed in the last section.

Dorner's work is important not only in that it shows the reasons people frequently fail in complex situations but also because part of his work helps us understand what people do that increases the likelihood of avoiding failure.

Throughout the book, we will come back to Dorner and the implications of his work on our discussion of PAR.

We hope that this brief discussion of the AR process has made you anxious to get started. But, before actual actions can take place or meetings can happen, we need to discuss the ethics of research and (if you are considering PAR) what to think of in building a participatory team.

Conclusion

This chapter has introduced AR and discussed the steps in the cycle. Hopefully, we have whetted your appetite and given you some ideas for projects that you might want to undertake. In the next two chapters, we focus on your proposal and your application to an internal review board (IRB) and give you a more detailed explanation with stories of how the three steps go together in your research.

Take Action

So, where do you go from here? We suggest you start by writing a list of possible topics for your AR. To do that, think in terms of what situations in your life you would like to help change. Depending on the requirement of your university, these might be situations in your business, nonprofit, or public administration office. Equally, they might be situations in your community or home life. We have seen graduate students undertake excellent AR on a variety of topics both personal and professional.

Additional Readings

Bate, P. (2000). Synthesizing research and practice: Using the action research approach in health care settings. *Social Policy & Administration, 34*(4), 478–493.

Bawden, R., & Zuber-Skerritt, O. (2002). The concept of process management. *The Learning Organization, 9*(3), 132–138.

Wicks, P. G., & Reason, P. (2009). Initiating action research: Challenges and paradoxes of opening communicative space. *Action Research, 7*(3), 243–262.

Chapter 2.
The Proposal and Ethics

Now that you have the basic idea of what AR and PAR are, as well as the steps involved and why you should use them, we will move on to some important ideas that need to be understood before beginning your own research project. The understanding of these basic concepts will help you create a solid research proposal, a necessary first step in an academic setting. There are some specific considerations you will need to be aware of when you are doing research in your place of employment or another location where you are considered an insider. As in any research endeavor, there are many ethical considerations that must be given considerable attention in order to maintain a quality research process that is fair and beneficial to all. AR and PAR develop as the project goes on, and this creates some difficulties in the planning stages as you can't always know where you are going, described by Herr and Anderson (2005) as "designing the plane while flying it" or by Reason and Bradbury (2008) as "building the road while walking on it."

The goal of this chapter is to get you past the difficulties we most often see in regards to proposals and IRB applications so that you might get on the road, or in the plane, with a solid foundation of ideas to support you. We will use the term *AR* to discuss elements that are common to both AR and PAR and use the term *PAR* when discussing elements that

People often say that research is a way of finding out what you are going to do when you can't keep on doing what you are doing now.
—*Charles F. Kettering*

have to do with the participatory group process. Remember, we take the somewhat uncommon but very practical stance that the elements of the actions in PAR are the same whether you have participants working with you literally from all levels of your stakeholders or whether yours would be closer to a team AR approach (for greater clarification, refer back to our discussion of participatory research in Chapter 1).

This chapter will address several questions:

- What are the seven key concepts in research writing?

- What goes into an AR proposal?

- How do I start to plan the proposal and my work?

- How can I avoid common mistakes?

- Am I doing insider research?

- What are ethical codes for research?

- How do ethics specifically pertain to the AR process?

- What are some specific ethical considerations when using a team approach?

- What are some potential ethical issues to consider in business, nonprofit, and public administration settings?

Reflective Questions

- ✦ What are your experiences with writing research proposals?
- ✦ Which do you think will be more efficacious for your research approach—AR or PAR?

What Are the Seven Key Concepts in Research Writing?

A solid structure requires a firm foundation. In research, your proposal is based on your understanding of seven research concepts (purpose, **scope**, methodology, findings, **conclusions**, limitations, and **contributions**) and how each concept works within the AR cycle of discovery, measurable action and reflection and the AR values of democracy, critical self-reflective practice, and professional development. We want to emphasize the need for you, as an action researcher, to package and communicate your findings within the framework and values of the scientific tradition in order to advance the integration of your insights into a broader research community.

Because, for many of us, research is not our entire lives, we have to come back to thinking in research mode from very different kinds of activities. These seven concepts that help reentry into doing research become easier. As an example, when called upon to write both the proposal and concluding paper for your AR study, listing these concepts helps to organize your thoughts and gives a structure to the paper or report you are writing. After this brief introduction, this chapter goes into more detail on how to use the seven concepts in your AR proposal.

Purpose

The purpose of your work is why you are doing it. Creswell (2009) states, "The purpose statement establishes the direction for the research." What you hope to accomplish may also be included in this section. The purpose is the driving force of any AR study because action towards a goal is an inherent part of the design. You may choose to mention in your purpose statement how your AR project advances one of the key tenets of the work, such as the democratic principle of all participants, and so on.

Scope

The scope is used to define your research plan. It explains the context for the study, the size of population, and the variables under consideration. Always make sure your scope fits the amount of time that you have to complete the work. Your proposal should not be for more work than you can finish in the allotted period.

Methodology

As we said before, methodologies are the overarching ideas that tie the actions taken to collect and analyze data together. **Methods** are the tools of research, quantitative or qualitative in nature and put together in a methodology (such as AR). When you align your methodology, you are telling others which ideas and constraints direct your work. With AR, you are saying that you intend to change the circumstances you are measuring as you go in order to influence positive outcomes. You also commit to working in a self-reflective cycle (qualitative by definition as you will use words to reflect) and being explicit about your discovery as well as your action or inquiry (data collection here is likely to be qualitative, but you may also find quantitative evidence important in your study). That does not mean you

Two students teamed to investigate how to improve the profitability of a small food kiosk. Through multiple cycles of work, they examined the books, set up a new type of accounting, and convinced the owner to stop giving credit to employees of the store.

are tying yourself to either qualitative or quantitative measurement; you can do both as you measure the outcomes of the actions you implement as part of your study. It is important to note that, within the academic tradition, AR is not experimental research.

Findings

Your findings directly relate to the data you collect. They are your assessment of what the data told you. Like conclusions, they are included in the final paper but not the proposal. As an example, if you are doing a pilot study to investigate what is needed to help your nonprofit grow, then you may choose to interview key stakeholders, which would be qualitative data collection. To understand what was said, you might open and selectively code the data to look for patterns of response (Strauss & Corbin, 1998). As AR develops in multiple cycles, sometimes what you are measuring is the success of one cycle compared to another.

Conclusions

The conclusion contains the author's ideas about the overarching meaning inherent in the data. They logically evolve from findings, but they do not have to have a direct connection back to data. This is the section of the final report where you, the author, tell your reader what you understand to be true and what you learned from your AR study. Discussed in more detail under ethics, your PAR study should not be published until all the participants agree to the conclusions.

The harder you fight to hold on to specific assumptions, the more likely there's gold in letting go of them.
—*John Seely Brown*

Assumptions and Limitations

All research is somewhat biased by the views of the researcher. When studying program X and how it might improve your business capacity, you have already made an assumption. You assumed that using this program will help improve your business capacity, which may be based on other experiences, perhaps, but ultimately is still an assumption. **Assumptions** are areas that you call to attention and then show how you have mitigated their effects. For instance, if you assume X, then you may ask a colleague to double check your data whenever you see evidence of X just to ensure your reading is not overly biased.

Limitations can include details on any ideas that you would like to implement but for which you do not have the time or money. You also may want to include other side topics that would be important under other circumstances but that you did not study. You could always ask more people, take your research to an international location, or have it continue for 5 or 6 years. Because you do not have the resources to do all of these things, you mention them as limitations. Discussed in more detail under ethics, the relationship you have with those you study may also provide limitations, such as a desire to include people in your study who are not available to you due to power issues within your organization.

Note: Sometimes you can get past limitations by rerouting or refiguring some aspects of your study. As an example, a man who wanted to study elements of data communication in the military was not allowed by his IRB to include people with whom he worked. He found that another division had similar issues and were agreeable to have him locate his study there. We suggest that, if you perceive particular types of limitations that you wish to get past, you discuss the specifics of the issues with your professors, who may have experience getting past some of the limitations you face.

Contributions

Contributions cycle the reader back to why and how your proposed AR study provides viable contributions to local, regional, even international contexts. Your discussion of how your AR project contributes should be related to your initially stated purpose.

You will be reading other people's research as part of your background discovery and literature review process. Some may be AR, yet other types of studies may also provide background into how others have approached topics similar to yours. It is helpful to also do a scan of blogs, social media, and websites to see where current trends are leading. It is possible that your study could add to the literature by validating or reputing a new way of approaching your topic.

It may also be beneficial for you to write a synopsis of the articles you have read by alluding to these seven concepts (for example, "The purpose of this study was . . ."). It will evolve to the point where you can read a piece of research, pull out the seven concepts, and understand the importance and comparative points of the research you read in a very short time, making your academic

Reflective Questions

◆ What are your thoughts on the seven concepts as a foundation for research?

◆ Can you begin imagining some of these concepts in a design for AR?

◆ Can you see how AR's stress on the process being tied to the literature helps solidify the basis for your work?

life easier. It also will be helpful for you to group your literature into subtopics so that you are clear on how the ideas weave together to form your thoughts that will drive your explanation of what you want to do. We coach our master's and doctoral students to use reference software and to put these abstracts or synopses under the *notes* fields so that they have handy reference to concepts in articles they may have read months earlier. Then, by sorting their references into groups, they can easily outline what they want to say in their review of literature. This not only helps the academic quality of your work but makes your final reporting easier as you have tracks back to the origin of your ideas.

What Goes Into an Action Research Proposal?

Formal research starts with a proposal. A well-written proposal makes both the research and the final report stronger because it forces you to think about some of the challenges you may face before beginning your project. When using AR as a methodology, you display your understanding of how the AR cycles (discovery, measurable action, and reflection) tie to the seven concepts listed earlier.

Rather than tell you about proposals, we will take each of the seven concepts and ask a series of questions, some of which may seem to overlap. If you answer the following questions and then restructure them into paragraphs, you will be well on your way to a solid AR proposal that you can then re-sort into the format required by your university. Appendix B is an example of how a student researcher answered the questions and Appendix C is his finished proposal.

Purpose

- What is your topic?

- What questions would you like to answer?

- Which of these questions will you have time to address in your study, and which will need to be placed in the *further studies* section?

- Why are these questions significant?

- What do you want to do, to accomplish?

- Why might others care about your problem?

- How do others see the same set of issues or problems? Back up your ideas with literature.

- Are there larger, overarching questions or issues that affect what you are researching?

- What values do you hold that will guide this work?

- How are those values in line with general AR principles?

Scope

- What is the context for this work, including the location, the environmental issues,

and the industry standards that create
the need to study your issue?

- What is the history of the issue in that
location?

- How many people are involved in the
AR project?

- What will be their level of involvement?

- What data already exists about the issue in
this specific location? Set up the reader's
understanding of the baseline from which
you are working. For example, are there
incident reports or gaps between policy
and actions that you can refer to?

- What population is affected by the issue you
are studying, and how will they be
involved in your research?

- What specific variable(s) will you be trying
to measure?

Methodology—Describing
the Action Research

- Will you be undertaking this project as a lone
researcher or part of a participatory group?

- If part of a group, who will be the other
participants, and what are their
stakes in the project?

- If PAR, then have you all agreed upon relative issues of working together? Rights of publication? Dissemination of results?

- How often will you meet?

Design (You May Want to Use Subheading for Each of the Action Research Steps)

- What do you need to learn before you advance to the action steps?

- How will the discovery be undertaken, and who will be responsible for what portions of the work (if done in a group)?

- What natural actions make sense for the first cycle of research?

- How will their outcomes be measured?

- What methods of measurement do you imagine using to gather your data? Note: Because of the evolutionary systems within AR methodology, we recommend a wide list of possible methods that can be honed later.

- What systems do you have in place to ensure accurate data collection?

- What protocols will you use for keeping reflective notes throughout the process? For instance, will you keep an ongoing journal?

We find no sense in talking about something unless we specify how we measure it; a definition by the method of measuring a quantity is the one sure way of avoiding talking nonsense . . .
—Sir Hermann Bondi

- How will you gain experience through active observation and reflection at the moment (reflective practice)?

- Will notes be taken at all meetings?

- How are these notes to be analyzed later?

Note: Findings and conclusions are not included in the proposal stage.

Ethical Assurances

- How will the rights of the people you study be protected?

- What are the rights of the people you are working with on a PAR team?

- What are your relationships with both of these groups?

- How will you ensure confidentiality?

- How will your data be protected?

- How will you work to ensure no undue pressure will be exerted by you?

- What are the options should people decide they do not want to participate?

- What assurances do you offer if they decide not to participate regarding the long-term ramifications of that choice?

Assumptions and Limitations

- What assumptions are you making as you start the study?

- What biases do you have about either the process or the outcomes you expect?

- What do you wish you could do that you will not be able to do?

- How long will your study be, and do you think you will have all the data you need to complete the study as intended? If not, then list the limit of size or time that makes your study possible, if not perfect.

- What other important things will you not have time to get to during this project?

Contributions

- What should people be able to do with the new information that will result from your project?

- How will your AR study contribute to your field?

- How will it contribute to your company?

- How will it contribute to the world?

- What are the implications of your work for the future in your field, your community, or your organization?

While every institution has its own protocols for research, there is a general consensus on what is required for a solid proposal. Answering the questions above and then using either the format provided by your university or the same format demonstrated in Appendix B should get you started on the formal research process. If you are working in a PAR group, then answering the questions above is an excellent exercise for the group as they undertake the project.

How Do I Start to Plan the Proposal and My Work?

Given all of this preplanning information, sometimes people still do not know where to begin. We have found it helpful to start in the middle and consider the measurable action that will be the heart of AR. Answer for yourself: What is it you want to do? Then, go backward to discovery (what do I need to know before I start?) and on to reflection (what protocols will I set up for my reflective practice?). These three questions work to break the inertia you may feel as you begin.

Glanz (2003) breaks down those basic three into a series of questions that we paraphrase here, which former students have found helpful to answer in getting started:

1. What unanswered questions would I like to see resolved?

2. What will I research?

3. What do I want to accomplish?

4. How will this study help my business, nonprofit, or public administration office?

5. What are my goals and objectives?

6. Can I reach those in the time I have?

7. Who will be involved in this study?

8. What are the logistics of the study—do I have all the access I need?

9. Do I have permission from my employer?

10. What actions do I expect to take?

11. How do I think I will measure the actions taken? What data will I need?

12. How will data be collected?

13. How will data be analyzed?

14. Who are my stakeholders?

15. What kind of a report will they need? (p. 54)

Note that you won't have all the answers to these questions at the beginning but that you need to keep your eye on the development of these answers throughout your project. Thinking about them at the front end though can show you where you need to advance in order to successfully complete your project.

How Can I Avoid Common Mistakes?

The following mistakes seem common for beginning researchers. We hope this list helps you avoid them:

Do

1. List everything that is needed in the area for ethical assurances (see the next section for more details). Some of the questions you will want to address include the following: (1) Do you supervise any of the participants of your study? (2) What informed consent procedures will you follow? (3) How will you ensure confidentiality? (4) How will you store data? (5) What kind of password protection will you use for data? (6) Are your study participants youth, prisoners, or members of other protected populations?

2. Write about the methodology as AR. During your discussion of the measurable actions, you may refer to the methods of gathering either qualitative or quantitative data. Many students display their lack of understanding of AR by going on at length on qualitative or quantitative data collection without discussion why AR is theoretically and practically important to their moving forward on a difficult question.

3. Read enough of AR theory that you can discuss whose ideas have influenced what you want to do with your project, how you will proceed, and what outcomes you are looking for.

4. Design ways in which you can engage in double-loop reflective and reflexive thinking (more on this in Chapter 3). A single-loop reflection is when you do something, reflect, and then do something else. A double loop requires that you also reflect on the governing or underlying ideals and responses that cause the outcome you saw. Double-loop reflections answer questions such as the following: What did I do? Why did I do it? What could I do differently that might make for a different result? After this type of introspection, an action researcher engages in new approaches to action (Argyris & Schön, 1978).

Do Not

1. Discuss the overarching problem that you want to address with this work when you only have 10 weeks of class in which to work. Remember proposals are specific to the time and resource level allotted for the work. The broader issues and work can be discussed at the end, perhaps in a section called *future studies*.

2. Describe your work by writing weak sentence stems such as the following: "I would like ..." "My goal would be ..." "I hope to ..." Then, write sentences that are more confident than you may feel about the strength of your work. Consider instead: "This study contributes ..." "The purpose of this study is ..." and "This research design ..."

Reflective Questions

◆ In reflecting on your answers for the questions that Glanz (2003) poses, what is the basis for your project?

◆ What do you need to do before you can answer the questions and begin your proposal?

◆ What other questions will you need to answer before you can start your project?

3. Predetermine every step of your AR project so that there is no room for flexibility or change as you proceed.

4. Plan your timetable without adequate time for analysis (see Chapter 7).

Am I Doing Insider Research?

What does it mean to conduct **insider research,** and what are the problems, challenges and rewards? *Insider research* refers to studies done by an employee on the organization that employs them. In the section on ethics below, we discuss the difficulties in conducting research in your organization when some of the people you will question are also those who report to you. There are other considerations as well; some provide opportunity for your research and others challenges.

In an article titled "In defense of being 'native': The case for insider academic research," Teresa Brannick and David Coghlan (2007) suggested that there are many opportunities allowed to the insider researcher that someone from the outside could never hope to duplicate. These include access to information, a preunderstanding of a situation and its history, and positive relationships with the people who will participate in the study. On the negative side, it is difficult to carry on research and equally continue your normal tasks as an employee; this duality can make you experience role conflict or send up hidden or double meanings to those around you. Organizational politics can seem to deepen or become more convoluted as you have to address situations from two perspectives. We will carry these thoughts further and discuss reflexivity in public administration in Chapter 3.

As previously mentioned, the purpose of AR is always to take positive action toward a goal that is perceived as being desirable. Whether or not we recommend insider research depends a lot on what your goals are. Brannick and Coghlan (2007) pointed out that few insider researcher academic papers get published in referered journals. On the other hand, we have seen huge organizational impacts as a result of some of our student efforts in researching and making a difference in their own organizations. One of the most spectacular examples was a project that culminated with the union and the management of the organization reconsidering how they implemented federal guidelines when it came to employee time off (Goff, 2009). In conclusion, if you want to have an outcome of this research be your own advancement in academic circles, then researching someone else's organization might be a good idea. On the other hand, if you want to make a difference where you work, then the fact that you are insider or native may work to your advantage. It is likely that the stakeholders will listen to you based upon your reputation within the organization.

Whether acting as an insider or outsider researcher, be aware of the constraints of your position, and do your best to maximize the potential. AR literature is full of examples where both positions have been used to catapult to successful implementation of new ideas.

Reflective Questions

✦ Is your current proposal that of an insider or outsider researcher? How do you think this position will work in your favor?

✦ What might be the advantages or disadvantages for someone starting this same research from the opposite position?

What Are Ethical Codes for Research?

Now that you know what you want to do, you have to consider the ethics of doing it. Ethical codes for research are broken down into principles (which guide your actions) and standards (which you are obligated to do by law). Looking to the American Psychological Association (APA) for guidance, we see five principles that inform 10 standards. These same principles form the basic guidelines for researchers (Beins, 2004).

Beneficence and Nonmalfeasance: Work to promote the welfare of others and do no harm. AR carries this a stage further by admonishing researchers to do good as well. Research is done primarily for the benefit of the participants and society. In every IRB application and documentation of informed consent, you are asked to explicitly list the benefits and risks to your participants (see Appendix G for an example). This documentation demonstrates the beneficence of your research design.

Fidelity and Responsibility: Promote trust through work that is a benefit to the community, taking self-responsibility and offering services to others as needed.

Integrity: Behavior promotes and ensures accuracy, honesty, and truthfulness in scientific inquiry.

Justice: Work to ensure that all persons have equal access and benefit from research outcomes and that none are held back or not involved due to bias or prejudice.

Respect for People's Rights and Dignity: Be aware of, respect, and promote the dignity of all persons, no matter what differences exist due to culture, age, socioeconomic standing, national origin, language, disability, or sexual orientation. Try to eliminate the effects of bias against persons in research.

We call your attention to the APA website at www .apa.org/ethics/ for more detail there. Other organi- zations of interest to businesses, nonprofits, or public administration on the issue of ethics include:

1. Society for Business Ethics: http://www.societyforbusinessethics.org/

2. International Business Ethics Institute: http:// www.business-ethics.org/links.asp

3. Association of Fundraising Professionals: http://www.afpnet.org/

4. National Council of Nonprofits: http:// www.councilofnonprofits.org/resources/ resources-topic/ethics-accountability

5. American Society for Public Administration: http://www.aspanet.org/scriptcontent/pdfs/ AboutASPA.pdf

Universities have strict trainings that will go into the reason proposals need to be subject to IRB hearings by helping you understand the history of human subjects research and why universities now protect the public from unscrupulous research designs. Prisons, hospitals, educational systems, indeed any public service agency will likely have strict protocols that will guide what you will be allowed to study.

One of the most important elements that ensures ethical procedures is informed consent. Here you, as the researcher, guarantee that every person involved in the study is informed of: the reason for the study, the benefits and risks they face by engaging with you, the ways in which you are gathering data from them, how it will be analyzed, and how participants may pull their data out of your study if they reconsider later. See Appendix G for an example as to what to include.

How Do Ethics Specifically Pertain to the Action Research Process?

Bear in mind that AR, PAR, and all their counterparts have at their cores the value of democratic principles and elevating the unheard voice during research. Therefore, all these practitioners are held to very high standards of behaving in a completely ethical manner. Greenwood and Levin (1998) put to voice what most if not all action researchers feel: "We see AR as central to the enactment of a commitment to democratic social transformation through research" (p. 3).

Let us go back to the three-step AR cycle and discuss it in light of correct ethical practices in research.

Discovery

Actions during the discovery process usually fall under the following three categories: (1) discussion data, (2) web research, and (3) archival. In discussion data, you explore what is currently true in your business setting regarding the issue you are studying. During web research, you look for examples of what others have done in similar situations. Finally, in archival, you investigate previous data from your organization or the public domain that may help you understand the problem or from which you can create a baseline for future measurable actions.

During the first activity listed above (discussion and exploration of your business), your private brainstorming or your group's discussion is ethical as long as you respect the rights of others and keep private information confidential. If you consider interviewing or doing surveys with your colleagues, then you move into the arena of human subjects. If this is the case, then you will have to ask for permission from the participants, allowing the data that they share to be used in your research. If your subjects are under the age of consent, they can give assent to be included in your work, but their parent or guardian will also need to give permission. The second or third activities listed above, looking for models or at archival data, do not involve human subjects and so are free of ethical considerations as long as you obtain permission to use the data or materials from people who own them or their copyrights.

Measurable Action

It is within the measurable action part of the AR cycle that most of the ethical considerations are found. For instance:

1. A student intended to increase awareness of the ethical practices within the large corporation with which his company had just merged; what happened instead was that his project created unrest.

2. A student concerned with communication difficulties charted interactions but was perceived by his colleagues as using his project to advance his own agenda.

3. A community project was launched to develop new administrative systems to aid in times of disaster. When the new systems became stalled in the public administration office, the community felt that their needs had not been heard.

4. A group of health care workers met and started an AR project to improve the quality of care in a nursing home. They were plagued with how to address issues in a small setting and to still protect the confidentiality of their clients.

5. A mid-level manager was also a graduate student. He wanted to use the project to improve the working relationship he had with his staff but was unsure about the power dynamics to

encourage the team to be honest about their feelings.

We will look at these one by one.

Maintaining a Positive Intention

Because AR is based upon the idea that people who are doing research often simultaneously want to create new and positive outcomes, we may assume that there are good intentions to promote the welfare of others and do no harm. This does not mean that no harm will result, or that you do not have to protect against harm, but only indicates that probably, at the outset, your ideal vision is to make a positive difference.

Accountability to Community

Inherent in the AR process is the intention to promote trust and benefit to the community; however, research is often looked at suspiciously by others. It is important that you not only make assurances that you are doing the right thing but that you establish protocols and hold yourself to a high level of expectation about your work. Part of working with fidelity and responsibility within the community is being amenable to answering questions and fielding concerns from interested stakeholders without defensiveness.

Integrity and Transparency

Integrity and what it means to members of your PAR group should be discussed openly at the beginning of the project. As most PAR groups will have diverse ethnic and cultural membership, it would be

We all should know that diversity makes for a rich tapestry, and we must understand that all the threads of the tapestry are equal in value no matter what their color.
—*Maya Angelou*

naive to assume that everyone will see the activities that lead to an ethical project in the same light. The more your individual AR or PAR project practices transparency in decision making, the more likely you will achieve the community buy-in that will make your project successful.

Integrity involves keeping records that authentically discuss the situation while maintaining the confidentiality of all who are involved and being willing and able to share the research process, not just the outcomes, with others. It also involves following through on actions and promises or, when that is not possible, being authentic and coming back to people so that they will not be disappointed.

Confidentiality and Respect for Others

Respect for people's rights and dignity requires that you are hypersensitive to concerns of others. This includes maintaining strict confidentiality of all your records, asking interview questions that are nonintrusive, and being willing to completely change your strategy if others or your PAR team find it in any way disrespectful.

It is important that the people from whom you gather data can rest assured that what they say will be referred to by others in a way that is completely anonymous. You must strip the story you are telling clean of all references that might let others in your community track it back to the source.

Grouping and analyzing data (aggregating it) takes the specifics of each case and merges them into

> **Integrity is telling myself the truth. And honesty is telling the truth to other people.**
> —*Spencer Johnson*

Action Research for Business, Nonprofit, and Public Administration

the whole of what you are studying. This will help improve your data analysis as well as add protection of your subjects. Your informed consent needs to assure your subjects how your records will be locked and whether you will aggregate all data.

Recognize and Address Power Dynamics

A simple and challenging component to doing AR is the power you may have over the people who you would want to include in your data collection strategies or the potential of misunderstandings concerning your research if they have direct report power over you. If you are a teacher, a supervisor, a manager, or in any way leading a group in which your subjects are involved, you must wrestle with how to ensure that all individuals are not intimidated by your questions or giving you the answers they think you want to hear. Likewise, employees must tread lightly when questioning their bosses. Power issues are so important that they will be discussed from multiple points of view throughout this book. Ethically, you need to consider that the person asking the question has more perceived power than the person answering—therefore, the people answering need to believe that no bad results will come either from their responses or their refusals to answer. If you are that person's supervisor, it is possible he or she will not believe your neutrality. Likewise, if that person is your supervisor, he or she may take exception to the momentary reversal of the "natural order" of power within your relationship.

Other kinds of power dynamics exist and should be considered in regards to your study. For instance, your institution may hold power within your community; certainly all offices of public administration have both subtle and explicit forms of power that may influence the degree to which people will give you honest answers to questions you want to ask. As an example, a new governor wants to understand how IT is being used in public offices and commissions an AR study. To what extent do you believe that those researchers will hear the whole truth as they conduct their study? Would it be more likely that each government office will first and foremost want to protect its access to resources?

Miller (2008) recommends that, in order to better understand the role power may play in your AR or PAR process and your ability to embed ethical principles in your practice, you should conduct an informal analysis of the power relationships within your setting. Consider which relationships and activities increase the effectiveness and empowerment of the communities or unheard voices within your study and which cause those voices to be silenced.

Reflective Questions

- ✦ What are your thoughts on the ethical considerations, and how can you apply them to your study?
- ✦ What would be the one ethical issue most likely to occur in your work?

Continuous Reflection on Benefit to Others

The reflective cycle can be helpful as you work to ensure that all persons have equal access and benefit from what you do. You can use the ethical principles as stepping-off places for part of your reflective practice, asking yourself and others whether and to what extent all people are benefiting as you might wish.

What Are Some Specific Ethical Considerations When Using a Team Approach?

Participatory Ethics

When researchers work in groups, they take on additional ethical considerations—these relate to how the five ethical principles above interact with their responsibility within, to, and as a part of the group.

Beneficence and Nonmalfeasance

Within the group, each individual researcher is responsible to keep the activities of the group to themselves and not disclose group dynamics or decisions outside of the PAR context. Each member is responsible to the group for active participation. As a group, the participatory team should discuss areas of potential harm to community members, which may be created by the research activity and how they might overcome those challenges.

Fidelity and Responsibility

PAR team members promote trust within the group by taking self-responsibility, by not speaking out of turn, and through regular displays of respect to all team members. Members act in trustworthy ways to the PAR team as they follow through on their commitments and timelines so that the project moves forward. As part of the group, every PAR member is equally responsible for services offered by, or the interactions of, others who are also part of the PAR team.

A PAR team investigating how to make medical practices safer for employees in a rural health clinic concluded that keeping confidentiality during research was a key element to success.

Integrity

PAR team members are honest, take and report data with accuracy, and work individually and cooperatively with integrity to the process, each other, and the community in which they interact.

Justice

PAR team members make sure no one is excluded from their group from offering data to their investigation or from receiving benefit from their work.

Respect for People's Rights and Dignity

PAR team members are respectful to each other and to members of the wider community, whether or not they agree or disagree with the mission of the research. They make whatever accommodations to language, culture, physical impairment, and so on, that may be necessary in order to gather accurate data in their investigations and ensure diverse participation in the process (James, Milenkiewicz & Bucknam, 2008).

In a final note of warning, Columbia University's "Statement on Professional Ethics, Faculty Obligations and Guidelines for Review of Professional Misconduct" (Teachers College at Columbia, 1986) as quoted by the University of Hawaii at http://www.otted.hawaii.edu/ makes the point as follows:

> In modern collaborative research, the implications of academic misconduct or fraud go far beyond the individual; they also affect collaborators whose own work has

been committed to objective search for truth. . . . Joint authorship requires joint responsibility; each author claiming credit for the entire work must also be aware of joint discredit. Investigators in collaborative research projects each must make reasonable and periodic inquiry as to the integrity of and processes involved in gathering and evaluating data. . . . Overall responsibility for the integrity of collaborative research rests with the principal investigator; senior investigators cannot be allowed to escape the consequences of the discovery of misconduct or fraud committed under their supervision.

What Are Some Potential Ethical Issues to Consider in Business, Nonprofit, and Public Administration Settings?

To some extent, all of the following issues may occur in each of the three settings: businesses, nonprofit organizations, or offices for public administration. We list them here only as general subcategories according to where we have most often seen them occur. We suggest to the extent that any of these concerns affect you, that they are fully considered prior to starting the project. You do not want to find yourself in a position at the end of the project where you either put yourself in some awkward situation or have to downplay your results.

Business Studies

Issues of supervision or engagement of coworkers was discussed in the ethics section. To some extent, participatory teams may minimize this in that all participants work together without role definition. Written agreements outlining the working relationships of the PAR team can be reached and should be kept on file. Specific clauses may say: (1) that all researchers are required to act in an ethical manner with customers and coworkers (maintaining confidentiality, etc.) but (2) that also there will not be negative repercussions because of disagreements or personal disclosure of ideas. For more information on the ethical issues involved here, see the business ethics associations listed earlier in this chapter.

Nonprofit Studies

Use of client data and the maintaining of their anonymity during conversations are ongoing issues. This can be aggravated when the nonprofit PAR team include clients. The group needs to be aware that, while many of them go home to other neighborhoods, their clients frequently live close by and know each other well, and a great deal of harm can be done through gossip. For more information, go to the ethical standards for nonprofits listed above.

Stakeholders who provide programmatic or organizational funds may be a consideration. Their concern will be with the outcomes of studies that affect the work they are funding, yet the PAR group and the organization's management need to consider what would happen if the team concludes with competing solutions. How will you ensure ethical reporting of data and outcomes when the message may not be politically correct? These issues are discussed in more detail in Chapter 7.

Public Administration Studies

Large data sets in the public domain (poverty data, health data) may have specific line items useful to your AR study. Be sure you use data to illuminate your issues and not to support your biases. As an example, a student wanted to work with state-level insurance data to investigate workers' compensation claims across the various state administrative structures that govern it. He found that these data alone would not tell the story. He decided neither to confirm nor deny the relative issues within states through phone interviews with administrative offices, asking them about their perceptions of whether a federally administered system would be more efficient.

Being politically correct versus being truthful can present ethical issues to public servants similar to pressure from funding sources to a nonprofit. Often, the tone of what is acceptable can change dramatically with shifts in the elected officials who will ultimately be stakeholders to the project as a whole. As an example, the way in which you ask a question about a sensitive topic (such as funding) will determine much about the data you have access to as a result. We will investigate these issues more as we discuss working with people in Chapter 6 and the difficulties of reporting on unpopular truths in Chapter 7.

Reflective Question

✦ In light of the setting you will be working in, what ethical concerns do you need to carefully consider prior to your study?

Conclusion

There are many things to consider as you pull together your proposal and IRB documents prior to starting your project. Because this methodology establishes the process through which action blends with research, the result can seem confusing. Keep in mind your purpose, the goal you wish to achieve, and then double-check as you go that all sections add up toward that outcome. Do likewise with the ethical considerations. Your goal is, of course, not to put anyone under undue pressure just to aid your research. As you write your IRB documents, consider what it would be like to be in their shoes and whether you agree that the benefits far outweigh the risks.

 ## Take Action

- First, be clear at the onset about the parameters of your topic. List what you want to know and which other interesting questions you will have to approach at a later time. This will help you stay focused on the phenomenon of interest throughout the research process.

- Next, discuss the elements of this chapter with your professor, who will undoubtedly have specific protocols, formats, or forms that need to be employed for both the proposal and the IRB.

- Then, set aside some reflective time, and go through the steps and questions, answering them and putting those answers into the proposal format set up by the university you attend.

- Read other peoples' AR studies (it is helpful if they are on a topic close to yours but not mandatory). Pull out the seven concepts, and write up a short abstract discussing the project's purpose, scope, methodology, findings, conclusions, limitations, and contributions.

- Develop your assumption and limitations section by answering the following questions: What are your assumptions about the successful outcome of this project, and how might it improve your business capacity? What bias do you have toward any one particular project outcome? What actions or expansions to your study would you take on if you had more money or time? As you do not have the resources to do all of these actions, mention the resources as limitations. Are there people who you would have liked to include but were unavailable due to ethical considerations? In what other ways is your project less than you might imagine its potential to be under other circumstances?

- Finally, a good portion of the proposal, especially the paragraphs relating to methodology, will be moved into whatever IRB format is required by your university. Because that is true, and before you actually begin to write your proposal, read Chapter 3.

 ## Additional Readings

Benn, S., & Dunphy, D. (2008). Action research as an approach to integrating sustainability into MBA Programs: An exploratory study. *Journal of Management Education, 33*(3), 276–295.

Doyle, P., & Brannick, T. (2003). Towards developing a food safety model: An insider research approach. *Irish Journal of Management, 24*(2), 38–54.

Lincoln, Y. S., & Guba, E. (1989). Ethics: The failure of positivist science. *Review of Higher Education, 12*(3), 221–240.

Chapter 3.
What to Do and
How to Do It . . .

At this point, you probably have some ideas of what it is you would like to study, issues you would like to address, and changes you would like to see made. You may even have written parts of your proposal. In order to move forward, you need some practical information on what it is you actually need to do in an AR project. This chapter will give you the detailed instructions you need to complete each step of the AR cycle. Finally, if you are considering using a team or PAR approach, then you will need to learn how to build a good participatory team for your project. As in the last chapter, we use the term *AR* for those items that serve for both and *PAR* for any considerations particular to the use of AR in either a team or participatory approach. Should you need to reference those considerations, we discussed participatory research in Chapter 1.

This chapter will address the following questions:

- What do you do when you do AR?

- What are the practical actions in each step of the cycle?

- What do you do in the discovery phase?

- What do you do in the measurable action step?

- What do you do for reflection?

A student wanted to help prevent diabetes in African American women. She discovered the lifestyle risks for the disease. She then wrote and distributed a survey. Data showed that women wanted the information even if they didn't have the disease. She proceeded to develop presentations and classes to meet this need.

- What is reflexion or double-loop learning, and what do you need to do to become a critically reflexive practitioner?

- What are some examples of action research projects that other students have done in business, nonprofit, and public administration?

- What did these students actually do in each of the AR steps?

- What is the best way to build a participatory or team effort?

- What are some tools that can make your AR project easier?

What Do You Do When You Do Action Research?

At this point, you know that there are three steps to every AR cycle and that there may be multiple cycles to an AR project, depending on the size and complexity of the issue and the time you can devote to it. Our students who have to complete the project in a single class often do either one long or two short cycles. This section will go over each step with an overview and then discuss what we have seen students do during each step. This should help you both get ideas and begin to plan.

As examples, business students frequently look at either their own business settings (see Chapter 2 for our discussion on insider research) or work to aid organizations within their communities. As an example, in our current class, we have business majors working with Big Brothers Big Sisters to aid them in finding male mentors for African American youth and with a green organization, helping them collaborate with others to spread their message in the community.

Students working in nonprofits frequently find the excuse to do a project for school handy as it allows them to research what their clients think of their services. We discuss one student who worked with his church on issues of retention. Other examples of student work include the following:

- Students in the military study the flow of products and services, communication, and supply chains.

- People in aviation study stress on the job.

- Health care providers frequently look for ways of improving practice.

- Public servants address how best to change their operations to meet the needs of a new administration.

- Students acting as citizens study how best to get the vote out on issues within their cities or towns.

What Are the Practical Actions in Each Step of the Cycle?

What Do I Do in the Discovery Phase?
We present the first step in AR as discovery because just the word invokes a sense of new possibilities. When life is full of new discoveries, we are open to

the potential of breaking past our limiting thoughts and taking on new ideas. Like explorers, the first step of AR reminds us to risk the unknown to come to the ideal of what we want to create. During the discovery process, you are generally looking for new ideas about what others have done in similar circumstances. This should include both published, recognized academic papers and a broad range of community resources.

Here are some hints that help the discovery process be exciting and invigorating (as all new learning can be):

1. Ask people in your community or business what they think of your project; collect ideas and opinions, then search the web for their validity in the broader environment.

2. Lay aside your assumptions about what you will find and explore web-based stories of people in similar situations, maybe in different industries, who have faced somewhat similar challenges.

3. Go several pages back in your browser search rankings; discover what tangential topics may be related to yours that you have not considered.

4. Do a library search on first your topic and then on other things by the same authors—what else are they involved in? Look in Google Scholar or EBSCO in your school's database. Look for both self-published and peer-reviewed documents to broaden your search.

5. See if you can find a web address for people whose work you respect. Write them e-mails explaining your ideas and your status as a

student. Ask them questions. They may not answer you—but it is just as likely that they will, and you gain access to discovering the thoughts of experts in your area of interest.

6. Whether or not you have decided to work in a participatory group, you can use part of your activities in the discovery cycle to brainstorm your ideas with others. Take notes, and then search the web for other phrases or connections that they suggest.

7. Search blogs for similar or related topics (http://blogsearch.google.ie/?tab=mb). When you find people blogging on topics interesting to you, be sure to comment—this too can start conversations that will help you discover new potential within your topic.

8. Do a similar search in websites such as YouTube, SlideShare, or Cooliris, and so on, to see if there are other types of media that relate to your topic, which will broaden the ideas you will consider.

9. Participate in forums on your topic or establish one in your virtual network (more on this in Chapter 6). Be sure to tell people you are doing research, and ask them if you can quote them whenever they share something that you may want to use later.

Keep notes or a log about what you are learning, and note the resources so that later, for the final report, if you need to cite and reference them, you can easily do so. When you feel ready to start to take measurable action, look over the log to notice and include any new ideas that will influence the measurable action step.

Discovery consists in seeing what everyone else has seen and thinking what no one else has thought.
—Albert Szent-Gyorgyi

The manager at a large company realized the project management software wasn't working. Her goal was to choose project management software that met everyone's needs. She discovered what the industry thought were the key concerns. She also interviewed staff about needs. The suggested software was shot down by the management, leading to the reflection that some opinions counted more than others.

Finally, in nonprofits and public administration, the consumer or client may well bring up issues of past treatment that require investigation by your AR project. This may require a short trip into hermeneutics or the investigation of archived e-mails, meeting minutes, or other artifacts to piece together previous organizational behaviors. These archival data may be the key to your discovery of past circumstances as they pertain to the story that started your investigation.

To further illustrate how the steps in AR work, we have included diagrams of student project steps throughout this chapter. In addition, you may want to consider the story of a businessman who asked, "Will participatory management work in a United States airline?" Utilizing a PAR team, his discovery step centered on finding out more about participatory management to uncover ways in which it could be or has been used. He also measured current practices and found "a festering matrix of poor communication, a general misuse of power that is producing an overall lack of trust and dissatisfaction with the way things were going in general; causing extreme low participation levels beyond any basic job duties" (Rose, 2010).

What Do I Do in the Measurable Action Step?

For measurement to be tied to action, you need to know the baseline, or where you were when you started, and that data has to be recorded. For many people, the first cycle of AR is exploratory. As an example, you may be starting from little or no knowledge or understanding of the things on which you want to have impact, and therefore, you may want to give a survey to your community to better understand the situation. The baseline would be X (little or no understanding). You would research the topic, and that would take you to Y (enough understanding to make a survey or ask a questions), then you would pass out the survey and get back the data that would take you to point Z. The measurement then is the distance from X to Z. The ability to make that measurement accurately and in a defensible manner according to research standards requires that you take notes (gather data) at points X, Y, and Z.

Our colleagues in Australia have said that sometimes an AR cycle can last a few minutes. We translate that to mean that they have experienced a natural evolution from a new idea into a short measurable action, as we have. As an example, you may be propelled to call upon someone you know in order to verify or discuss something you uncovered in discovery—this could be seen as a measurable action because you first ask questions and then can measure the growth in your understanding as a result. It is not so important what you call your activity but that you keep your eyes on what you are discovering and doing and that you keep protocols for your reflections.

Some hints that help the measurable action process be defensible and concrete are:

1. Keep a three-column log. The first column records the date. The second contains a description of what you did. The third describes the result. You will quickly find that your big cycles are made up of lots of little measurable actions.

Reflective Questions

✦ What are some ideas you have about where to look for information on the Internet?
✦ Who are some people you can contact in your discovery phase?
✦ How do you plan to organize and document your discoveries?

A public administrator was unsure if the systems in place for disaster worked. He wanted to help public servants be more prepared for disasters. Discovering literature outlining the types of difficulties during disasters, he then surveyed all the workers in one section. There, he found confusion in roles and delivery of services. After this, he reflected on the good systems present but also the need for training.

2. Keep your eye on the purpose of your research—what it is you intend to do. You may want to draw a diagram with your baseline at the bottom and your purpose at the top. Write in activities as they make sense somewhere along the scale from beginning to where you want to end up.

3. Ask everyone in your participatory team to keep this kind of record, and start every meeting with a discussion of the measurable actions people have taken.

4. Ask AR virtual network members to jointly maintain a forum thread solely focused on measurable actions. Everyone should be invited to post there regularly.

Let us continue with the story of the student studying the airline he worked for. As mentioned earlier, he was investigating to what extent participatory management was apparent in his workplace and where it might be considered. In order to verify his team's strong opinions, they took action and measured company communication against variables such as honesty, kindness, and justice, which had been established in the literature as those that equate to high moral and ethical values (Ketola, 2006). By measuring and correlating the ideals of corporate culture against words used in company communication, his team reported, "Just having had the words justness, generosity, etc. in their work life increased their morale at work" (Rose, 2010).

Figure 3.1 outlines the way in which a student filled in his action process log by laying out his actions and his results week by week.

My Action Process Log		
Date	**What I Did**	**The Result**
First Week: Discovery	Arranged meetings with key stakeholders to better understand their concerns on the issue.	New directions for discovery result, how others have overcome these same hurdles.
Second Week: Discovery	PAR team meets and serves as inspiration and "center of creativity" for main student researcher.	New research ideas are generated
Third Week: Discovery	AR research is read and diagnosed as to the ways in which they measured outcomes.	Student also met with protagonist about the issue.
Fourth Week: First Measurable Action	Student met with the man he reports to. They discuss ideas and discovery steps to date.	Student receives positive feedback and the permission to move on.
Fifth Week: Action	Lots of actions are taken in the form of meeting with the representatives of all the stakeholders...	...but nothing results
Sixth Week: Action	More meetings...	...but still no results
Seventh Week: Measurement	Finally the project yields results:	Major stakeholder agrees to host meetings to escalate the new ideas and obtain permissions to institute change.
Eighth Week: Reflection	In final reflection the student researcher sees:	1) the planned seminars could not have happened without the deep discovery cycle, 2) having the data from other organizations was one of the convincing factors that helped change the minds of the stakeholders.

Figure 3.1

What to Do and How to Do It . . .

Reflective Questions

✦ What time management issues could come into your use of the action process log?

✦ If involved in a PAR project, how will your group merge reflections and logs?

✦ What project management protocols will you use to stay on track?

What Do I Do for Reflection?

There are two main parts to the reflective step of the AR cycle. The first is the internal process where you make meaning of what you have discovered and done, and decide what you want to do next. You want to keep your final report in mind, so it is helpful to develop a protocol for regular reflection (one possibility is discussed at the end of this chapter and Appendix A). Remember, this is the portion of the research around which all the other parts circle. Wicks, Reason, and Bradbury (2008) point out that, in their review of AR literature, authors frequently report the "importance of practice and life experiences and these as integrated with—and often preceding—philosophical, political, and intellectual underpinnings" (p. 15). Reflection and reflexion, both of which are covered in this section, become the central hub for those levels of understanding.

The second part of reflection, and the one that is somewhat critical to a university-based project, is your reflection on the role of the literature in your project development. For instance, let us suppose that your topic area is virtual leadership. You have used your library and found several research articles on virtual leadership, some of which have influenced your ideas and actions. Keeping the final report in mind, as you reflect on what you are learning, you tie it back into the literature that is influencing your thought. This should be done in such a way that you capture the citations and references as appropriate. The logic model discussed at the end of this chapter (and included as Appendix D) can be used to keep this type of reflective note.

Some hints that help the reflection step be of the most use to you in your final report include the following:

- Set up a protocol for regular reflection about each part of the AR cycle.

- Assign reminder notices to your calendar to ensure regular reflection throughout the AR process.

- If you are working in a PAR group or virtual network, set up protocols for sharing reflections and determining group consensus of what has been going on.

- Ask yourself: How do I really feel about how it is going? What could I be doing differently? What actions have I taken? Is this getting me where I want to go?

- Ask yourself how these ideas and what you are doing compare and contrast with things you have read. Make notes of the similarities and differences.

- Finish a reflection cycle with a list of next steps that you intend to take.

To finish the tale of our student researcher, upon reflection, he found that participative management is a good idea and its values would change the culture and improve morale. The PAR team quantified the benefits they found in morale from working with him on the project to be a 15% increase in team participation, averaging a new trust level of

31% overall. The desire to participate in their work beyond their required duties had risen.

What Is Reflexion, or Double-Loop Learning, and What Do I Need to Do to Become a Critically Reflexive Practitioner?

To go deeper into personal practice, not just as an action researcher but as a person in business working for nonprofits or in public administration, a practitioner needs to also develop ways and means to question his or her own behavior. Writing reflexions (how you respond to the situations you face as part of your research) is the key to this level of personal investigation.

To survive, you naturally build up habitual responses, but without being regularly questioned, these become prejudice, bias, or at the very least, behavioral traits that are taken for granted. Awareness of one's self is a precursor to work in AR and requires a degree of objectivity as to relative emotional intelligence (EI). EI is defined by Goleman (2006) as a set of competencies and skills that entwine four main positive human abilities: self-awareness, self-management, social awareness, and relationship management. Cunliffe (2005) makes a striking case for the fact that professionals wanting to boost their professional skills (especially the soft skills of collaboration that are so necessary in modern work environments) require both self- and critical reflexivity.

In Chapter 2, we discussed double-loop learning, where you not only act, reflect, then act again but act, reflect, and question your underlying motives, then reflect on what they mean to your behavior, and then act again (Argyris, 2002a; Argyris & Schön, 1978). Cunliffe (2005) and others who support reflexive work point out that merely working a regular reflective protocol into your work can indeed help to drive new kinds of practice but rarely touches the personal elements that ultimately control whether and how much any change initiative will work (Fletcher, Zuber-Skerrit, Brendan, Albertyn, & Kearney, 2010; Jones, 2010). Reflexivity requires that we suspend the part of us that wants to drive home an effort at change, recognize our own human fallibility, and open to meditative space to see if the deepest part of our natures can become more apparent and offer deeper insights. This may seem ethereal in light of *bottom line thinking*, but actually, it is touted as necessary in fields as diverse and education, social sciences, and economics, where self-reflexivity is often seen as a precursor to truly ethical and democratic action (Freire, 2000; Spiller, Erakovic, Henare, & Pio, 2011; Wiedow, & Konradt, 2011).

Reflexivity in business may cause you, the researcher, to question issues of power within the organization. Are certain people or clients given special privileges? Where is there evidence of truly democratic ways and means of addressing situations and where are all decisions developed top-down? Where does your position as researcher in the hierarchy color your answers to these questions? What would someone above or below you in that hierarchy answer to the same questions? If you and the entire organization were operating from the highest ideals of human behavior, how would things change?

Reflexivity in nonprofits frequently focuses on the treatment and inclusion of clients. Where is the organization functioning as a charity, doing things for or to others as determined by historical patterns? Where is there evidence of collaborative problem solving that includes the population that is addressed by the mission of the agency? What evidence exists that the organization is meeting its mission? Where might you, as a researcher, have a positive influence? Where are you driven as a result of your position within the organization, and what might others say if they were addressing the same concerns?

Cunliffe (2005) develops critical reflexivity for people in public administration from a postmodern philosophical stance of critical theory, which requires that all assumptions, underlying motivations, and postulates of one great truth for all people are questioned. Also suspect is the use of inclusive language with little or no evidence of participatory work to obtain those claims. Her stance is that, especially in public administration where staff doing AR are in insider positions, the focus of AR is to help in the administration of the laws equally for all people, staff, and administration who need to develop reflexive thinking and to develop reflexive protocols. The focus of outsider research in a similar situation may be to point out errors in the administration of laws to correct them. Figure 3.2 lays out how a student used critical reflexivity and reflection to increase

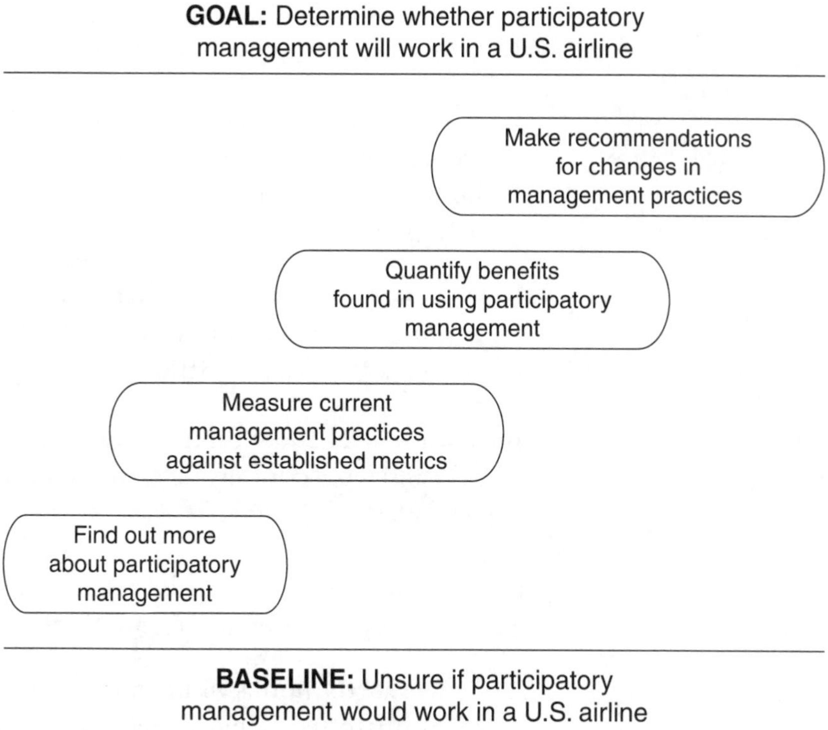

GOAL: Determine whether participatory
management will work in a U.S. airline

Make recommendations
for changes in
management practices

Quantify benefits
found in using participatory
management

Measure current
management practices
against established metrics

Find out more
about participatory
management

BASELINE: Unsure if participatory
management would work in a U.S. airline

Figure 3.2

his understanding of himself and the process
throughout his AR cycles.

But, what do we really do to become self-reflexive?
The starting base is to objectively look at your relative level of emotional intelligence across Goleman's
(2006) four constructs:

1. Asking questions as to whether, in any given
    instance, you were acting from your highest
    consciousness in the best interests of everyone
    concerned or merely reacting to outside circum-
    stances (self-awareness).

2. Asking whether your actions positively influence a fair and equitable outcome (self-management).

3. Asking whether your behavior models what you would hope for as that which creates positive norms of behavior on a societal or even global level (social awareness).

4. Asking whether people involved leave feeling as though they were respected and that their concerns were heard (relationship management).

Then, you will take your practice to what Cunliffe (2005) considers a critically reflexive level when you begin to ask the following:

1. What are the limits of my knowledge and of the norms of practice in my organization?

2. Where are the norms within my organization that work to keep some in power over others?

3. To what extent do our clients hold a different reality about this situation than we do?

4. Are any positions, ethnic or cultural ways of looking at the world, or socioeconomic situations disrespected as a result of any of our organizational practices?

5. What do we assume we know about our clients and the issues they face?

6. Who has more power in the organization than others? On what is that power based, and to what extent does it shut down the potential for others?

Action Research for Business, Nonprofit, and Public Administration

7. How do my colleagues and I respond when considering the possibility of power inequities or change?

8. What causes defensiveness, and what underlying assumptions drive that reaction?

9. What activities or rules are never questioned?

10. What assumptions am I making about the stakeholders or other participants in my project, about myself as a researcher, or about the outcomes we desire for the project?

Students interested in delving more deeply into issues of reflexivity are encouraged to investigate the work of Argyris on defensiveness in organizations and to search on keywords that include *reflexion, reflexivity,* and *praxis.*

What Have Other Students Done Across the Three Business Sectors?

Throughout this book, you will find examples that outline different students' AR projects conducted over 8-week periods. These examples include what sectors they were working in (business, nonprofit, or public administration) and the topics of their AR projects. The examples also sometimes include brief descriptions of what they did in each step of the cycles they completed. Taken together, these examples show the breadth and depth possible with AR in just a few short weeks.

The student projects presented in this book range from the selection of project management software

Reflective Questions

+ What timing and format will you use in your AR reflective protocol for this project?
+ What questions that help lead to self-or critical reflexion were most appropriate for your situation?
+ Can you think of other avenues for reflexive discovery that are appropriate to your project?

A regional resource manager had to address the question of whether to support biofuel across five counties. He decided to research the cost-effectiveness of a biodiesel fuel cooperative. He discovered costs from municipalities for the previous year and met with stakeholders to engender support. The figures he received showed cost-effectiveness for local revenue generation. The result was a cost-effective solution for fueling transit that was also good for the environment.

to improving African American women's knowledge about the risks of diabetes. Other examples of student work include: improving risk management in a manufacturing plant, diversity in the aerospace industry, and investigating participatory management in an airline. One student researched the need for an improved communication system during emergencies for special needs clients, and another worked on improving an inventory system in a family-owned business.

These students discovered things such as the following:

(a) the assumptions of their employees as to how things work,

(b) the importance of tone in departmental e-mails and communications,

(c) some shortcomings in business systems and people in their organizations,

(d) and, the transformational potential of AR.

Measurable actions ranged from asking questions of stakeholders to completely revamping organizational systems. Some students used surveys, and others used interviews to gather data. Some students even created their own measurement tools specifically designed for their projects.

Reflections are often about power, the need for AR, and shortage of time. Reflections sometimes focus on the topic of the AR project and other times on the actual workings of the project itself. Sometimes, the reflections indicate a positive resolution to the initial problem, and other times they indicate newly discovered problems or issues.

What Is the Best Way to Build a Participatory or Team Effort?

Some of you have decided that the best way to proceed would be with a team or, better yet, to include your clients, customers, or other people in your wider stakeholder group, bringing them to the table as equals with you in your research. While there may not be hard and fast rules for building a PAR group that supports you, there are general guidelines you may want to consider. PAR is both a team and more than a team-based approach to research. On the simple level, working in a PAR group brings up all the same issues as are common on other teams, and so we start this section with some reminder notes on basic team process. Yet in its best moments, a PAR team brings the unheard voice to the table in a democratic moment of equality—the funder, the client, the "other" is given a voice, not only to be heard but also to share in the process as equals. We will cover those issues in the section below.

What Counts in Team Building?

Building great-working teams to help solve problems is not hard as long as all the participants care about finding new and sustainable solutions to the issues at hand rather than advancing their own opinions about what is necessary. One painful

In light of the perception that his church was losing members, a local pastor wanted to increase retention of his congregation. PAR added ideas, but the research would cost him time. To lessen the impact on his time, he implemented a web-based survey. On it, he found that situations are different in other parts of the world. This led him to start an outreach program.

Reflective Questions

✦ Which of these student examples is most interesting to you and why?
✦ What new ideas do you have after reading these examples?

example illustrates our point. In the 1980s, there was a wave in Colorado of philanthropic organizations demanding collaborative work when they funded causes. One such organization generously set up collaborative teams all over the state to make a positive difference in teenage pregnancy but demanded that all the points of view in the communities were represented on the task forces they funded. One team failed completely when a major abstinence-only organization sent representatives who stayed only as long as it took to adopt the point of view that there would be no condoms distributed, then they stopped showing up for the meetings. They were not interested in building diverse solutions that served the whole community but rather in having their opinion win (Easterling, Gallagher, & Lodwick, 2003). Therefore, look for people who are flexible and willing to work, are willing to learn, and will seek a number of viable options targeting solutions to your issues.

We think that diversity becomes the second most important consideration in a great team. Every human context brings with it both wisdom and blind spots. A great functioning PAR team includes diversity among these outlooks. As an example, one team based in a school wanted to develop new practices for students experiencing frequent moves due to homelessness. One of the members of their team was an old-time citizen of the neighborhood. He was concerned that they did not know enough about where these children lived or their impact on the entire community, and so he mapped the

Action Research for Business, Nonprofit, and Public Administration

locations of low-rent apartments. This ultimately led to having a nonprofit organization design a neighborhood-based community service. Without his point of view, all the services would have likely remained within the school. Diversity of team members may include culture, age, outlook, position, and organizational differences.

Finally, look for team members who are committed. The student story in this chapter of the man who was investigating retention for his church was a sad story for the student. Every meeting, he had a different group of people who would come, thus creating delays in his project because steps had to be repeated to catch everyone up.

What Are the Optimal Numbers of Players?

How long will your project run? The longer the project, the more people you should recruit at the beginning as you will experience a natural attrition due to competing responsibilities or transfers, diminishing the number who can attend. A long-term project will need to have a number of members who have the historic memory of the entire project.

On the other hand, there can be difficulties getting a large number of people scheduled to meet, and fewer numbers may mean having well-attended meetings. People need to know that their time is an important contribution to the whole. As a facilitator, it will be your task to ensure that everyone's opinion is heard.

Teamwork is the ability to work together toward a common vision. The ability to direct individual accomplishments toward organizational objectives. It is the fuel that allows common people to attain uncommon results.
—Andrew Carnegie

How Should You Include Various Stakeholders?

Many kinds of people may be stakeholders for your project, some of whom you should consider asking to be part of your group. These groups may include your customers, clients, or others who benefit from your work, or those that have control over it in some way (the public, legislators, owners of your companies, etc.). In many business settings, these are also people from within your organization who hold different positions as they relate to the topic of your research or in the hierarchy of staff positions.

Start with some reflexive practice (as discussed earlier in this chapter). Who are your stakeholders? Who embody the unheard voice or represent views that you know are not included yet in your project? How much power do they have over you and the project? How interested would they be in your results? How much do you trust their ability to be flexible? The answer to these questions determines to what extent you offer stakeholders active participation in your PAR team or how often you report your results to them. There are no right or wrong answers, but stakeholders have power to support your results or squash them, so planning from the beginning to elicit their help brings long-term, sustainable results.

Asking the "other," in whatever form these differences may come, to your table as a participant in your research is a bold move and one that, when handled well, can help your research rise to the top.

To make it work, though, some human concerns must be addressed: How are you going to be able to convince them of your sincerity? What is in it for them from their point of view? What guarantees will you be able to offer that this will not be a waste of their time and resources? Finally, do they impress you as a person as someone who is willing to engage with you in the reflective and reflexive process without defensiveness (or being willing to work beyond defensiveness) on both sides?

Once you believe you have identified stakeholders who will add to your project, you need to invite them to do so. Be prepared to share your hopes and dreams and to listen to theirs. It has been our experience that these relationships fall into three camps, the most rewarding being when, together, you can share the human side of what you do. A solid working relationship will still be workable if both of you are invested in the outcomes and show up on time to get your mutual work done.

Intergroup hostilities may arise and tie to our later discussion in Chapter 5 about power dynamics. The tradition of AR recommends embracing the resistance and moving toward the concerns to listen actively to alternative views. Active listening frequently allows the richness available in opposition to emerge. If all points of view have been explored and still no release of tensions is apparent, then we recommend you seek advice from your professor and consider canceling the work while looking for another alternative, such as gathering data and cross-checking points of view in individual interviews. As the facilitator, it is your responsibility to clarify the expectations of the group, allowing participants to come and go freely depending on if those expectations will allow them to commit to their participation. Remember in tense situations that the guiding light is the principle of beneficence, covered in Chapter 3.

What Facilitation Skills Should You Keep in Mind?

A successful PAR group is characterized in two ways: active participation by the majority of people involved (although the specific people involved may shift over time) and effective decision making. We will consider each.

Active participation depends on to what extent participants are invested in finding answers to the questions you are asking and solutions to the problems you are addressing. It is their responsibility to examine their personal contributions and whether they believe their input will be meaningful and a good investment of their time. They may not have much time and may be concerned that, once the group starts to find solutions, these will involve more work than what they are willing to commit to. The trick in facilitating these issues is to discuss them with participants prior to the first meeting and then ask the group to discuss them during the first meeting. Also, be sure to use techniques such as the tossed salad method quoted below to ensure that everyone contributes right from the beginning. Those who do not contribute will often be the first

Teamwork is no accident. It is the by-product of good leadership.
—John Adair

to leave the group. The following can be used for any task that needs group input.

> Tossed Salad: Place a large bowl on the table. Give out small slips of paper and ask everyone to write down one idea per slip, putting them in the bowl. When people have finished writing ask someone to mix up the slips. Pass around the bowl so that each person can take out as many slips as they tossed in. Go around the table and have them share ideas before discussing and refining the most promising ones together. (Bens, 2008, p. 55)

Effective decisions are those that efficiently create results, costing the least in time, energy, or resources while moving the AR project forward in measurable ways. Consensus is great but takes time to build, and not every decision requires it. For instance, if your group has a selection of options, the members may decide to divide into subgroups, each working on the solutions that appeal to them. Prior to taking off on their own, all the team members should agree on which measurements they will consider evidence of success.

The no vote is the winning vote in those situations that demand consensus. For example, consensus should be used when deciding what to publish in final reports on the project. Baseline rules for participatory research are that all members ethically need to agree on the final report because all their names will be on the document as authors and so their personal integrity stands behind what is published there (see cautions from Columbia University in the previous section on ethics).

How Do You Maneuver Past Known Obstacles or Political Issues?

As we have presented throughout the book, Chris Argyris (2002a) used double-loop learning and reflexive practice to help overcome defensiveness, which along with power issues, make up the myriad of personality disputes that derail AR projects. Fortunately for the student, the short time allotted by classwork seldom brings these to a critical level. Obstacles that have to do with lack of access to resources or materials held by those in power are discussed throughout AR literature, being as they are a mainstay of the long history of AR in increasing democracy in situations through listening to the unheard voice. We will come back to this in Chapter 5 where we talk about working with people and groups and when we discuss the complexities of power as they play out in AR and PAR. No matter what obstacles you face, honesty is the best course of action, with a sensitivity to both the expected and potential unexpected outcomes of your work. You want to surf the fine line between your integrity and honesty and not cause harm to others. Situations may call for: (a) early debriefing prior to publishing results, (b) group meetings to discuss ramifications of your actions or findings and how to defuse any potential outcry (even the best results will have those who don't support change), and (c) publishing positive outcomes in such a way as to gather support or, conversely, in such a way as to continue public debate.

These are situations that frequently have silver linings. It is often when, through disagreement, we reflect upon the subtleties of power and personality that we rise above both and add truly wonderful out-comes to our own lives as well as to AR. It is best to keep in mind the potential for reaching beyond the focus on improving techniques of practice to address the broader questions about how work influences the context in society, becoming a vehicle for critical debate to improve our world. As we discuss in Chapter 8, AR achieves its full potential only when we reach beyond where we are and toward a critical view of what causes the obstacles we face, better able to speak for the needs throughout our businesses, nonprofits, or offices of public administration.

What Tools Are Useful for Action Research Student Researchers?

Chapter 3 has outlined how to proceed with the different AR steps and what students have previously accomplished using AR for class projects. To conclude this chapter, we offer you a couple more tools.

Action Research Reflection Tool. This is a simple form (see Appendix E) that has all three steps, and our students find it useful for weekly reporting and reflection during the AR process. In its simplest form, you just give yourself three headings on the page: Discovery, Measurable Action, and Reflection. You keep it on your desk and make notes, writing them up once a week as a log. We find that sometimes it is hard to know where to put a given event. Do not worry about it; you can always re-sort the items later. What it does is give you is a form where, by tracking the steps week by week, you will later have the data you need to

Reflective Questions

- ✦ Do you feel confident to run a participatory team?
- ✦ If so, what seems exciting or holds potential? What are you nervous about?
- ✦ What support would you need to make this a viable option in your circumstance?

Nothing has such power to broaden the mind as the ability to investigate systematically and truly all that comes under thy observation in life.
—Marcus Antoninus Aurelius

document what you discovered, what steps you took, and their outcomes. Your reflections will often lead toward the conclusion section of your final report.

Action Research Logic Tool. This form helps tie literature to action and measurement and has been found helpful by students for organizing their thoughts and actions. While the use of the logic model is outlined in more detail in our first book (James, et al., 2008), we introduce it here to help you merge your literature review with your discovery process for the purposes of academic defensibility. The first column is your research question for that cycle (they may change as your project goes on), and in the second column, you list the citations of other work that was influencing you. The third column lists the variables or ideas from that author that are of interest. In the fourth column, you note what you can do to measure those ideas in your setting, and in the fifth, you note how you will analyze your data (most likely coding if qualitative and one of several statistical tests if quantitative). Qualitative and quantitative issues are covered in more depth in the next chapter.

 ## Conclusion

In this chapter, we have gone over what it is that you will actually be doing in your AR project. We have covered the practical steps to be taken in the discovery, measurable action, and reflection stages of your project and given you examples of projects done by other students. These examples should have given you a good idea of some of the possibilities that are out there for you in completing your own AR project. If you are planning on using a participatory approach, we have included some tips on how to build the best team possible. Finally, in this chapter, we have presented several tools that are available to help you in successfully completing your own AR project.

Take Action

You are now well armed with ideas, so the next step is to take action. This might include the following:

- Calling others and getting a team together.

- Investigating if the business you want to work with has research protocols for permission, filling out the forms, and submitting them.

- Enrolling the help of a librarian in your web research for your discovery step.

- Making up the forms you need so you are ready to capture ideas as they come to you.

- Doing a literature search to locate experts whose work focuses on the same issues you face—and writing them e-mails to ask key questions related to your project.

Additional Readings

Daley, A. (2010). Reflections on reflexivity and critical reflection as critical research practices. *Affilia*, *25*(1), 68–82.

Fengning, D. (2009). Building action research teams: A case of struggles and successes. *Journal of Cases in Educational Leadership, 12*(2), 8–18.

Jakubik, M. (2008). Experiencing collaborative knowledge creation processes. *The Learning Organization, 15*(1), 5–25.

Prinsloo, M. (2008). Community-based participatory research. *International Journal of Market Research, 50*(3), 339–354.

Chapter 4.
Methods and
Measurement

The end goal of doing AR, whether in an academic environment or other context, is to do something that has measurable results. The essence of AR is the blend of both action and research, using the reflective cycle to then delve deeper into the issue you are facing, which spins you off into another cycle. A secret to having measurable results is to plan ahead, and that requires a general understanding of methods and measurement. We started this chapter by asking students what their questions were about methods and measurements. Those questions constitute the substance of what is discussed here.

Chapter 4 will address the following questions:

- What types of methods are there, and which are most commonly used in AR?

- Can you tell me more about qualitative measures?

- Can you tell me more about quantitative measures?

- What about mixed methods?

- How do I know which method(s) to employ?

- What are some examples of methods used by other students?

- What if I can't figure out how to design the data collection and analysis for my research?

What Types of Methods Are There, and Which Are Most Commonly Used in Action Research?

The two basic types of methods used are qualitative and quantitative, which sometimes are mixed and both of which can be used singularly or together in AR. Qualitative is concerned largely with understanding the lived experience of people, while quantitative research is largely concerned with exploring causal relationships, proving hypotheses based on theory through the use of experimental design. Qualitative works with words and helps you understand all the human motivations behind what you are studying, while quantitative measures with numbers and helps you get an idea of your topic across a broad range of people. Both require your time in different ways, although qualitative analysis, when well done, doubles or triples the time it takes to collect data as you code and reflect upon it. We believe you should carefully consider these basic methods before deciding which to use in your study. Much will be determined by: (1) your connection to the people (your sample population) and (2) how much time you have. It is important that you plan enough time to interact in relation to others as you mutually work to improve your practice, the conditions you face, or the quality of some aspect of your life. Table 4.1 may help with your initial decision-making process.

Table 4.1

Method	Qualitative	Quantitative	Sequential Mixed Methods
Use it when you need to:	Understand the lived experience of people. Allows you to question a few people about their perceptions and understandings.	Explore properties or causal relationships to prove or to disprove a relationship or theory. Allows you to question a lot of people's general perceptions about an issue.	First develop and then confirm information on your topic. Allows you to either question the smaller group to advance an idea that the larger group will confirm or deny or vice versa.
General data collection process:	Develop questions. Ask them. Probe for more definition.	Develop questions and scales for answers. (1) Test them. (2) Rewrite them. Continue 1 and 2 until your tests confirm the efficacy of your questions to your topic or population. Distribute your instrument to the population of your study.	Develop qualitative questions or quantitative instruments as appropriate for which type of investigation will go first. Proceed with that investigation. As data are collected and analyzed, develop the alternate form of question. Implement the confirming data collection.
General data analysis process:	Read the data completely. Sort into themes. Count instances of words. Code for specifics derived from literature. Read out of context by code. Develop new ideas or theories about the topic.	Collect data. Analyze it using appropriate tests of frequency. Run statistical analyses.	Analysis proceeds, first one and then the other as per the descriptions to the left. The relationship between the qualitative and quantitative evidence is also considered using all available comparison techniques.

We develop the idea that AR as a methodology and philosophy (Elliott, 2006) employs the idea that you should do what works. AR is not exclusive of any format used, and this is a large issue as it can be very difficult for you to remain philosophically and theoretically true to two sets of research tasks, philosophical ideals, and theoretical boundaries. Toulmin (1996) reminds us that our methods must be appropriate to both our subject matter as well as the context and the needs of our stakeholders. Building on that theme, Ospina, Dodge, Gabrielle and Haofmann-Pinilla (2008) discuss the difficulties in using a hybrid design as containing challenges to the researcher on several fronts. First, you will need to consider where the theoretical frameworks, the research focus, and methods in which you are interested differ. As an example, AR's cyclic nature may require that data collection be varied across cycles as the work progresses. When you write it up, how and to what extent do you discuss the research theories that drove your choice making as one discussion or per the chronological timeline on which you made those choices? Ospina and colleagues found the greatest difficulties with issues of when to let go of control of the inquiry to those who would, under other methodological philosophies, be seen as subjects in the research rather than coresearchers. If you choose a participatory design for your AR project, you too may face these issues.

It is helpful to remember that, in all other research methodologies, action and inquiry are separate from each other—first, someone does the research, and then others, often a whole new set of people, act upon those findings and conclusions. This is one of the issues at the heart of what makes AR different. Yet, as a researcher, you will also need to be able to claim credibility, validity, and reliability. For that reason, in this section, we provide a very brief overview of qualitative and quantitative methods. We will also mention some of the considerations you may consider when deciding what methods to use in your own AR project. Each of these methods

Action Research for Business, Nonprofit, and Public Administration

will be explained in more detail in the coming sections.

The utilization of both qualitative and quantitative methods includes a set of practices for data collection and analysis that have been proven over time. The adoption of these methods aids the AR researcher in producing valid, credible, and reliable results. One of our reviewers reminded us:

> One couldn't use a deductive process that included a control group, dependent and independent variable along with an identified treatment and call it Action Research; nor would one create a survey and apply it to a scientifically identified random sample and then analyze the results with the intent to generalize it to the population of interest and call it Action Research. You might though decide with your participants that a particular approach is worth attempting in an effort to get the desired results. To test this you may use a survey that you then quantify through appropriate statistical analysis, which would represent qualitative research with quantitative methods that are nested in the research design. (Anonymous Reviewer, 2011)

Action researchers use both types of methods in their studies, although we find that students see the most useful results when using qualitative methods with small populations.

Qualitative methods add body and life to data similar to how the drawing in Figure 4.1 uses the analogy of animals adding active life to the rocks and trees of the forest. Rather than manipulating numbers, you ask people directly for their perceptions of the world. Collection methods include: interviews, focus groups, observations, and a researcher's personal reflections. Studying issues qualitatively involves the collection of thoughts through words or pictures. Creswell (2009) sets up a logical progression for thinking through the issues of qualitative design and reporting on it. He recommends that the researcher start with the purpose of the study then move to the research questions you are trying to answer. From there, the data collection techniques must fit their subjects. Finally, you report to others how you analyzed your data, what coding techniques you used, whether you had others look at it to determine if they agreed with your findings (intercoder reliability), and so on.

Quantitative methods, on the other hand, collect data as numbers (for example, human resource personnel development instruments, questionnaires, or surveys). These methods are used to

Alan Bucknam | Notchcode | 2011

Figure 4.1 is a whimsical portrayal of how qualitative methods might be seen as adding body and life to raw numeric data.

Action Research for Business, Nonprofit, and Public Administration

extract information from a large number of people and to run simple or complex statistical analysis, highlighting the frequencies and relationships in which difference variations occur (Creswell, 2002, 2003, 2009; Gorard, 2003, Nelson, 2002). Once again, Creswell (2009) gives us a progression that will help you think through the issues of using quantitative measures: First, you state the problem, then you develop your hypothesis of what you think is true and its reverse statement, a null hypothesis, or what the opposite would be. You develop or use an existing instrument that you give out to as large a population of people as you have available. You need to take into account whether a random sample is needed and how you would do it if it were. You collect your data and analyze it in such a way as to give you information on whether your hypothesis or null hypothesis is the truth as seen by the sample of people you questioned.

Can You Tell Me More About Qualitative Measures?

We live in a world where everyone has an array of thoughts about how things should be done. This multitude of ideas, opinions, and beliefs generates qualitative evidence both rich and confusing. As action researchers, we sort through and implement qualitative data collection in numerous ways. These include conversations, notes, e-mails, voice mails, interviews, focus groups, and our reflective data. AR holds itself to the standard of being responsive to the organization in which the researcher is based. Therefore, qualitative data collection will in some part be a component in an AR study.

Table 4.2 Qualitative Data Collection Methods

Data Collection Strategy	Attributes	Challenges	Set Up & Tools
Data collected directly in words from people.			
Interviews: one-on-one question-and-answer sessions where the researcher may use a variety of techniques. Interviews average 30 to 60 minutes per person.	Reveals information about the worldview of a single individual. This is a flexible strategy that (with care) can be massaged during data collection as needed to heighten results.	Interviews are a time-consuming form of data collection. To gather data from one persona requires preparation, the time of the interview, and the time of transcription.	Recording device, note-taking either on paper or digitally, Smart Pens or some digital transcribers might be considered to bridge the voice/digital gap for analysis.
Focus groups: groups interviews using the same variety of techniques and taking approximately the same length of time as interviews.	More time effective than interviews but with slightly less flexibility. The group process may encourage results from shy or hesitant people when the group brings up topics with which they agree.	The group dynamics may interfere with complete or accurate data.	Same tools used as for interviews, but we recommend a second person to act as recorder as you facilitate the group discussion.
Data collected once or throughout a process of change.			
Reflective journals: handwritten or verbal accounts of an event or group of events over time. These often unveil how writers subscribe meaning to their topics.	Subjective account of the event from the point of view of the writer, who may be the researcher or a subject of the research. Can be collected once or throughout a process of change.	Similar to interviews, reflective journals display the worldviews of single individuals. They also frequently require transcription.	Individual records can be collected in a journal or digital reflective note format. Recommend adhering to a calendar to guarantee regular note-taking.
Field notes: written explanations or data taken often by multiple observers at a single event, capturing interactions of interest to the larger topic under study.	May follow a prescribed format or be open-ended. Generally gathered by the researcher or PAR team and therefore likely to target the topic of study.	Somewhat more objective than reflective data although still subject to the biases of the writer.	Set up observation protocol prior to event. Chart the attributes to be studied on the left column and delineate the people or events along the top. Some measurements can be checks for seeing it happen, while others demand explanation. Leave space for notes. Consider videotaping if permission or ethical structures allow.

Action Research for Business, Nonprofit, and Public Administration

Table 4.2

Data Collection Strategy	Attributes	Challenges	Set Up & Tools
Data collected during the event(s) being studied.			
Anecdotal evidence and logs: data taken from people often outside the research team that report the facts of the interactions as understood by the writer.	May follow a prescribed format or be open-ended. May be more objective about the topic of study because it's not constrained by the biases of the PAR team's discussions of the topic under study.	Somewhat more objective than reflective data although still subject to the biases of the writer. Generally not gathered by the researcher or PAR team and therefore may not center on the topic of study.	If possible, set up protocol in which evidence is given. This encourages similarity across informants.
Observations: stylized note-taking about predetermined portions of an event or group of events under study, generally taken by more than one observer. Observations often tally the number of times an event takes place.	Are often collected over a period of time. Can be collected by a variety of people, thereby increasing the possibility of reliable results. Accuracy may be helped by voice or video recording prior, with multiple people taking part in analysis.	Accuracy may be constrained by the point of view of the person recording the data.	Set up observation protocol prior to event. Chart the attributes to be studied on the left column and delineate the people or events along the top. Some measurements can be checks for seeing it happen, while others demand explanation. Leave space for notes. Consider videotaping if permission or ethical structures allow.

People experience circumstances differently. In order to hold your AR study to a standard of rigor, you must collect and analyze the data in a systematic way. You start with your question, then you systematically collect all the data that might have a bearing on that question, then you systematically code the data to extract meaning. We'll go through those steps one by one.

Gathering Qualitative Data

Table 4.2 outlines the categories of qualitative data collection methods.

Figures 4.2 through 4.5 offer visual representations for these ideas.

Analyzing Qualitative Data

Qualitative evidence, when rigorously analyzed, makes it possible for action researchers to uncover, expose, and consider the complexities within their organizations. Many researchers subscribe to the notion of "living with your data" because qualitative data analysis is much more than coming out

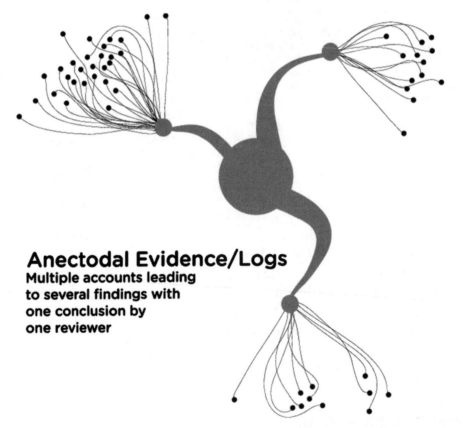

Anectodal Evidence/Logs
**Multiple accounts leading
to several findings with
one conclusion by
one reviewer**

Alan Bucknam | Notchcode | 2011

Figure 4.2 offers a representation of gathering anecdotal evidence and generating findings, leading the researcher to arrive at a central ground or a conclusion.

Action Research for Business, Nonprofit, and Public Administration

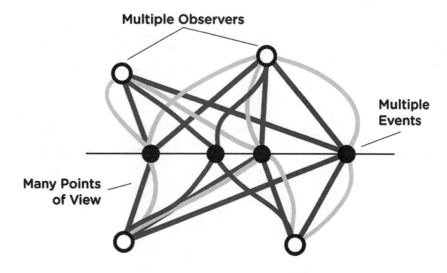

Multiple Observers

Multiple Events

Many Points of View

Alan Bucknam | Notchcode | 2011

Observations

Figure 4.3 shows how observational evidence from multiple observers and of multiple events gives perspective on a subject. A team of researchers all participate in multiple data-gathering events, bringing their own spins to their observations. Their team meetings allow them to debrief and arrive at similar conclusions, which then (like the black dots) add up to the understanding developed through the AR project.

of an interview with an understanding of what has been said. These data require continual review to unleash your subconscious mind, thereby allowing the development of new meanings or theories about the work. While no other kind of scientist would endeavor to measure a situation with an infinite number of questions or variables, this is precisely what businesspeople doing AR do when investigating their organizations. These layers of complexity may require you to go through multiple cycles of analysis and reflection to unpack relationships that will advance your work.

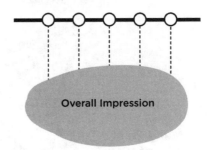

Observing an Event Over Time

Alan Bucknam | Notchcode | 2011

Figure 4.4 points out that, while observing an event over time and gathering an overall impression, it is important to remember that no singular event will allow you to experience enough to develop a concrete or credible explanation of events or circumstances.

Qualitative evidence extracts depth and adds body to your conclusions about what is going on in your situation. Data collection and analysis tools are employed as you try to delve deeply into circumstances and understand the motivations involved. Because motivations are as complex as the circumstances that engender them, it's important that you analyze the data from multiple viewpoints to collect the full range of potential meaning. These data are particularly informative when viewed from the perspectives of:

- **Meaning:** the significance of situations (held in people's minds as meanings) is subjective and varies depending upon personal experience. More than any other type of

Action Research for Business, Nonprofit, and Public Administration

**One-on-One Interviews
Lead to Deeper Answers**

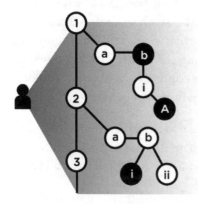

**Focus Groups are Less Flexible
but Encourage Participation**

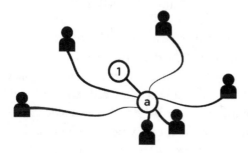

Alan Bucknam | Notchcode | 2011

*Figure 4.5 portrays how one-on-one interviews
yield more depth but are time-consuming;
focus groups are more efficient at drawing out
hesitant interviewees but are limited in scope.*

query, when you ask someone else what
something means to him or her, you receive
answers that give you insights into motivations
and other deeply personal attributes.

- **Context:** the background and current situation of the people and the circumstances you study influences understanding. This is true whether it is a personal context (e.g., age, gender, or cultural background) or a business context (size of company, location, industry, norms of behavior, etc.).

- **Historical viewpoint:** the history, past situation, and actions that led to the current situation need to be understood and reported.

- **Causal relationships:** The study of causal relationships requires a strong chain of logic with a wide range of diverse opinions collected and analyzed at each link in the chain (Maxwell, 1996).

After gathering a range of qualitative data, you then read and reread the data using various viewpoints or perspectives. You might start by doing simple counts of how many times certain words are used and begin to identify themes. When you see particular phrases of note you code them, which involves marking each with a color or note. You want to code or devise a way in which all the similar codes can be separated away from the body of words in which they were originally embedded so that you can read all of those remarks one after another out of context. You also take notes in some way so that later you can reorganize the data according to those notes. Strauss and Corbin (1998) and their brilliant work on grounded theory taught us to read and reread our material until the relationships between items that came up for interest start to become clearer. They suggest

Action Research for Business, Nonprofit, and Public Administration

that qualitative researchers first *open code* their data, reading through it without looking for any particular outcome, coding what seems interesting. You then reread it and *selectively code* your data, looking for evidence suggested likely to be present by your previous discovery review of the literature on your topic. Your search is designed to find both similar and divergent ideas. When consciously mixed with analysis from various viewpoints, you greatly increase the chance of finding ideas that would never have occurred to you if you merely took your data at face value without analysis.

Where Do Reflective and Reflexive Practice Fit In?

In our experience, most businesspeople believe themselves to be reflective practitioners. Sagor (2000) defines reflective practice as looking inward each day so that "reflections on the findings from that day's work informs strategies and outputs for the next day" (p. 7). Adults believe that they are reflective, but what they mean is that they think about their work and occasionally discuss it with others. What we mean by formal practice is a regular protocol for note-taking that addresses what happened in every given period of time in terms of discovery, measurable action, or reflection. Building the habit of a regular reflective practice is a mainstay of AR and may be best engaged in when in response to others. Reflective practice has four parts: first, debriefing what has happened; second, reflection on thoughts and feelings; third, reflection on possible next steps; and finally, brainstorming new possibilities or ideas. Table 4.3 outlines some basic types of reflective questions that might

Table 4.3

	Business	Nonprofits	Public Administration
Debriefing what happened	Steps taken to design a new business product	Steps taken to improve mission-oriented services	Steps taken to improve customer service
Reflection and our role in it	Did it go well? What could be improved? What new lessons developed? Are there more people whose input is necessary? Was our leadership adequate? What about our role could have been improved? What instances point to our success now or in the future? What do we still need to do or understand?	What changes can we attribute to our new actions? Did our clients respond well? If there were negative responses, what did we understand from these? Did we prepare people for the change adequately? Were we well prepared ourselves? What instances point to our success now or in the future? What do we still need to do or understand?	Was the implementation successful? What could be improved? Are changes needed in documentation or forms? Was communication among staff efficient? Was the customer satisfied? What evidence do we have of satisfaction? What about our role could have been improved? What instances point to our success now or in the future? What do we still need to do or understand?
Reflection on thoughts and feelings	How do we feel about this circumstance? What do we feel good about? What improvement would we try to implement next time?	Will these actions advance our mission? What do we feel good about? Where do we seek improvement next time? How do we feel about our client response?	How do we feel about these changes? Do we believe that they will both make our work more efficient and our customers happier? What do we feel good about? Where do we seek improvement next time? How do we feel about our client response?
Brainstorming next steps	What help do we need to be more successful? What information do we need to collect? What steps should we take? How will we measure the success of those actions?	Who should we call in to help us dig deeper or provide a more efficient implementation plan? What information do we need to collect? What steps should we take? How will we measure the success of those actions?	Do we need more customer feedback? Should we develop a plan for ongoing improvement? How will we keep measuring our outcomes? What next steps are indicated?

Action Research for Business, Nonprofit, and Public Administration

be asked by students in each of the three categories of business, nonprofit management, and public administration. This is meant to begin your questioning process. Of course, most instances will overlap among the three categories of readers. As an example, customer service will be similar in the other types of business activity.

One of the things that makes AR different from other research methodologies is that research

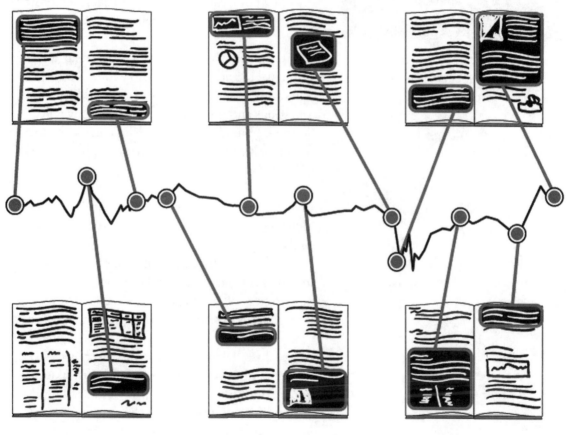

Figure 4.6

Alan Bucknam | Notchcode | 2011

"Converting it into data demonstrated the functional value and has made a believer out of me."
(Rossi, 2010)

practitioners look to their reflective practice notes and crunch them as qualitative data. This particular habit was very important to David Rossi (2010), a Midwestern banker who said, "My biggest take away was the functional benefit of using qualitative data from journals and meeting notes in a qualitative manner. Journaling was new to me and didn't come easy to a few of us (men). Converting it into data demonstrated the functional value and has made a believer out of me." Figure 4.6 illustrates how journals and meeting notes can be converted to data, demonstrating the functional value of reflective practices.

His sentiment was echoed by another man, a principal in another study who wrote, "I asked questions about how to improve and clarify data, questions and other technical issues in my reflective journal. I found reflection helped narrow the focus. It also helped me recognize that this process works" (Drobney, 2005).

It is important here to come back to the similarities and differences between reflective and reflexive practice and to encourage both. When you are in action, you can still open up to your intuitive understanding of the moment and adjust your behavior to enhance the opportunity of meeting your ideal. A negative feeling may guide us to realize something is off, and we adjust.

Critically reflexive practice embraces subjective understandings of reality as a basis for thinking more critically about the impact of our assumptions, values, and actions on others. Such practice is important to management education because it helps

Action Research for Business, Nonprofit, and Public Administration

us understand how we constitute our realities and identities in relational ways and how we can develop more collaborative and responsive ways of managing organizations (Cunliffe, 2004).

Reflection happens after the event and so does not lead to direct adjustment at that moment. It does allow the long view, however, where an analysis can be made of where you are versus your vision of what you want to be (Coghlan & Brannick, 2005). Reflection brings in the power of data and merges it with subjective response, increasing the likelihood of success. Reflecting on your reflexive practice increases your critically reflexive responses and your business practice overall.

Can You Tell Me More About Quantitative Measures?

Quantitative measures surround our daily lives and are recorded everywhere in our world. From the weather, to the percentages of kids doing well in school, to the likelihood of any candidate being elected, quantitative data help measure an unpredictable universe giving it the appearance of being solid and predictable through the display of evidence. Quantitative measures are excellent at giving us snapshots of what is happening within large, even huge, populations as we search out the relationships between attributes or the causes of attributes. The census is an excellent example of that, where we may see changes in demographic populations within communities, changes of education and social economic status, and so on.

Reflective Questions

+ What is your current experience with collecting qualitative data?
+ How do you see qualitative methods as being helpful for your study?
+ What do you think would be the difficulties in using qualitative methods for your study?
+ What three things can you do to increase your reflexive practice and marry it to your reflective protocol?

In general terms, quantitative data answer questions about how things are, or how people perceive them to be, the relationships between attributes or the causes of situations. As mentioned in the beginning of this chapter, when we believe that we have an idea ourselves of how things are, the action researcher develops a hypothesis that he or she believes is true. Quantitative data are excellent to prove or disprove that hypothesis.

Gathering Quantitative Evidence

At a practical level, action researchers or PAR teams are most likely to implement questionnaires or surveys to either confirm or deny qualitative evidence they have already gathered. Surveys are methods of asking questions with a predetermined range of answers. The methods most often employed in AR studies include both written questionnaires and verbal surveys of the subpopulation on a particular topic. These techniques often query the people we work with, or our clients, about either their experience with or ideas about situations in our companies. Researchers tabulate and summarize the answers in frequencies, which offer a snapshot of people's opinions across the wider community at a particular point in time. The quantitative methodology allows businesspeople to understand the characteristics, opinions, attitudes, or previous experiences of groups within their environment.

These data collection and analysis techniques include methods that classify (demographics as an example) or address questions (such as who the clients are). To verify perceptions of the populations we study, action researchers develop surveys where people may answer multiple choice or Likert-scaled questions that demonstrate where their ideas are along a continuum of possibility. Examples of such scales include the following: "On a scale from 1 to 5, with one being the least and five being the most" or "Mark the degree to which you agree with the following statement from 'not at all' to 'completely.' "

When surveys are well written and tested prior to implementation, they reliably test the opinions and perceptions of a larger group, which could not be reached by qualitative means. Building good questions free from both vagueness and redundancy is the challenge of survey question writing. It is not enough to say that questions are: (a) brainstormed, (b) written, (c) tested by a diversity of people who comment on them, and then (d) rewritten and reformatted for easier completion. Good questions are carefully designed and provide consistent measures in comparable circumstances (Fowler, 2002). Therefore, AR practitioners need to focus on designing statements and questions to accurately measure the information they are after, not as they would a document written in a more conversational format.

The issue arises regarding question reliability, which means whether people in similar situations respond to a question in identical ways. Several problems impact question reliability. First, in a population's primary culture, people intuitively learn to view events from different perspectives; therefore, the same questions will mean different things to people from different cultures. Second, people's memories of past incidents diminish with time; therefore, surveys about recent events will have greater accuracy in results than if you are questioning the past. Third, respondents will tend toward vague answers rather than specific ones, so your questions need to be as definite as they can be to measure the finite accurately. Finally, ratings will mean different things to different people so that reliability of answers will be increased if you offer explanations of the scales you use. What some respondents rate as good, others rate as fair. The goal, for all these distinctions, is to "ensure consistent meaning to all respondents" (Fowler, 2002, p. 81). In other words, in order for your research questions to be reliable, you have to have had considered and tested them with these issues in mind.

Other issues you need to watch out for are population validity—in other words, are you asking your questions of the right people (Sapsford & Jupp, 1996)? Who fills out your survey determines the answers you will receive and therefore the credibility of your study. Securing the right population takes several steps: First, you need to define the population and the subsets it contains. As an example, it may be important that you question both young and old, managers and staff, or people with diverse ethnic backgrounds. You then organize these various subsets into a sampling frame or graphic organizer that holds various records such as the subpopulations you will search for, their relative percentage within the larger group, and so on. Then, you need to decide how you will select a sample representative of that frame. There is a statistical guarantee that, if you select your sample randomly, the probability is that your answers will be significantly close to those you would receive if you were able to ask everyone. The difficulties in producing a random sample is outside of the scope of this book, but caution is needed and a plan put in place at the beginning of a study if this is a tactic you want to pursue.

Sometimes, action researchers are lucky enough to have their study follow along the same line as other research, and they can make use of standardized instruments. These instruments have the advantage of having been pretested for reliability on the measures they wish to study. There may be a cost involved in implementing such instruments, however.

Quantitative Data Analysis

Researchers no longer need to spend hours calculating data using complicated formulas. The statistical techniques required by most AR academic researchers are readily available with computer software. This text is not meant to go into any of them in detail.

When asked which methods researchers selected most often to analyze quantitative data, we find that it depends on what they want to do with the evidence. Nevertheless, when action researchers need to characterize populations and or the result scores they use *descriptive statistics,* which include the following:

- Median—the middle of the data as if sorted on a line, separating the highest values collected from the lower values at the midpoint.

- Mean—the average score, computed by adding all the scores and dividing by the number of people who answered the question or took the test.

- Percentages or frequencies—measures of the frequency within the overall population that answered a question in a given manner reported as a percentage of the whole.

- Standard deviation—measures how much the scores deviate from each other or the range of the scores occurring from the center point. This is reported both in figures and as a chart showing whether and to what extent any particular score falls within one standard deviation of the mean.

It is important if you are designing your own survey that you mock up some potential data and practice how you might report them. As an example, if what you need to show is whether or not the majority of your population responds in a certain way, then you may want to use a four-part Likert scale rather than a five-part scale, which would not as easily report a simple majority (because respondents have the option of selecting the neutral answer in the middle). With some practice, you can design a simple yet effective way of gathering data from the people around you that easily translates to a report that has meaning for your stakeholders.

What About Mixed Methods?

Creswell (2009) leads our discussion on mixed methods as his work also incorporates evaluative time-study techniques, which are particularly

Reflective Questions

- ✦ What is your current experience with collecting quantitative data?
- ✦ How do you see quantitative methods as being helpful for your study?
- ✦ What techniques will you use to increase the reliability of your questions?

important in AR studies, because you will likely want to measure the effects of your actions over time. Time is an important element throughout mixed methods for a number of reasons:

1. Intent—as an example, your intent may be to gather a little data and then test it through alternate methods or, the reverse, to test a little across a lot of people and then delve deeper into what proves to be the most important or interesting. Are you exploring new territory or looking to explain situations that are already in place?

2. Your schedule—it may not be possible to adequately collect both kinds of data at the same moment.

3. The relation of the data to each other— are they meant to confirm findings and conclusions or to show alternatives?

4. How do these data collection and analysis cycles merge with and support the AR cycles?

Sequential exploratory strategies are often employed by AR and PAR with the intent to uncover basic human motivations behind a situation with qualitative evidence, the key points of which will later be confirmed or denied across the wider population by using a survey. The survey assists in helping the researcher understand their earlier data.

Examples of sequential exploratory work already mentioned in stories in this book include:

- When both the risk management specialist and health care managers explored when their safety guidelines were not followed, in which contexts, and why in order to make improvements.

- The public health care nurse first surveyed the parents of children with special needs about their concerns regarding emergency situations and later interviewed them as to the specifics to design a database for emergency providers.

- The public gymnasium manager and Pilates teacher who first surveyed and then interviewed her clients in order to improve her program.

How Do I Know Which Method(s) to Employ?

In comparing methodologies, qualitative research starts with the research question and quantitative research starts with the hypothesis, but AR starts with a desire to get something done. As you progress toward getting things done, you will likely have both questions and hypotheses that you will want to answer or test.

For example, say you start by wanting to make your human resource department more inclusive in its practices. You would have both a question and a hypothesis:

- You might question the following: What are the best practices for recruiting a diverse workforce? To answer this, you might interview a number of human resource officers in different companies.

- You also might hypothesize that your company does not hire a very diverse workforce. The methods you would need to study that would be quantitative as you would go through company files and crunch of numbers of applicants, demographics, and who was hired.

Because AR projects are often done in academic environments, students can be limited on time. Therefore, more should be said about the endgame or data analysis comparison in order to facilitate good planning. Both qualitative and quantitative methods can be time-consuming or relatively quick,

Qualitative Data   **Quantitative Data**

Alan Bucknam | Notchcode | 2011

Figure 4.7 illustrates that qualitative data may appear simpler on the surface, but reveals deeper meaning upon examination. Quantitative data may be more immediately visible, but care must be taken to approach data collection in a way that serves the best interests of the research.

depending on several factors. It is a good idea to carefully think through the details of your project and make sure you will be able to achieve your desired results considering the time and resources you have available.

Qualitative data takes a while to analyze. While the surface understanding is apparent at the time of an interview, a body of evidence requires contemplation and review. First, people's words need to be transcribed and resorted, then examined, and re-examined for similarities and differences in meaning and tone. This step provides rigor, helping to ensure that personal biases or selective hearing do not flaw analysis. The use of software can aid a researcher in extracting meaning from qualitative evidence, although many techniques can accomplish similar analysis by hand. Although qualitative methods can be time-consuming, this can be counteracted by only studying a very small population. In other words, you could choose to interview just a few key people or hold a couple of focus groups in order to make sure that you can accomplish your project in the time you have allotted.

In contrast, quantitative data can be relatively quick to analyze. Perhaps for this reason, many students immediately decide they will just do surveys, thinking this will be the easiest and least time-consuming method. What many students don't understand is that the success of a survey is highly dependent on the quality of the survey instrument, which can be more difficult than it seems. Quantitative methods require planning and diligence up front to ensure that the instruments are in place when the researcher intends to gather evidence. What appear to be well-developed questions may hold many meanings in the multiple choice answers. If questions or answer choices are misunderstood by the respondents, the resulting data are useless. A well-crafted, reliable survey ensures that the respondents do not feel coerced to provide the answers they believe the questioner wants to hear. So, in reality, coming up with a survey that will produce useful results can be a very time-consuming and intense process. In order to counteract this problem, a researcher can decide to use a survey that has already been tested and proven to be valid and reliable. In order to accomplish this, the researcher would need to peruse the literature to find a proven instrument that measures what this researcher is looking to measure. Once quantitative evidence has been gathered, a researcher may need software equipped to crunch the numbers for a variety of tests.

There is power in using multiple methods, especially when time only permits looking at a small population. Creswell (2009) points out three difficulties for the researcher when using mixed methods: the amount to extract data collection, extra time to analyze both text and numeric data, and the requirement for you to be familiar enough with qualitative and quantitative forms to do a good job of both.

Table 4.4 summarizes some of the factors you may consider when choosing your methods.

Reflective Questions

+ How might your population size and time constraints affect what methods you choose?
+ Ideally, what type of method(s) are you considering for your research and why?

Table 4.4

Method or Data Collection Techniques	Pros	Cons	Circumstances	Time	Possible Costs
Qualitative	Extracts the depth and richness of the human experience. Allows for flexibility during the research process.	Generally limited to a small population.	Great for exploratory research when you have little knowledge of the range of human experience that surrounds your topic.	Questions can be designed quickly. Data collection and in-depth analysis can be time-consuming. This can be limited by picking a small sample	Recording device if desired. Analysis software if not doing analysis by hand.
Quantitative	Uses scientific methods to gather information using an appropriate sample that can be applied across a wide population. Allows the researcher to collect a broad range of data across a wide population.	Understanding is limited by the instrument used. There is no, or limited, ability to probe deeper.	Good when you have very specific things you want to measure. Allows for correlation analysis between variables.	Unless pre-verified instruments are used, survey creation and testing can be time-consuming. Depending on the volume of data and the experience of the researcher, data entry can be quick or time-consuming. Analysis is generally quick.	Paper and copying fees if doing a hard copy survey. Web fees if doing an online survey. Software for data analysis.
Mixed methodology and evaluation of program implementation	First gathering personal qualitative data and then testing it across the broader population through quantitative methods has much to recommend it. Checks and balances allow for a greater cross-check of findings.	Every new step takes time. In order for program evaluation data to show evidence, several sequential data collection points need to be included in the study.	Useful in circumstances where precision counts and where stakeholders are swayed by really good data. Also good when there is adequate time to dedicate to the study.	Mixed methods and program evaluation take the most time.	Any of the above.

Action Research for Business, Nonprofit, and Public Administration

The Qualitative Method

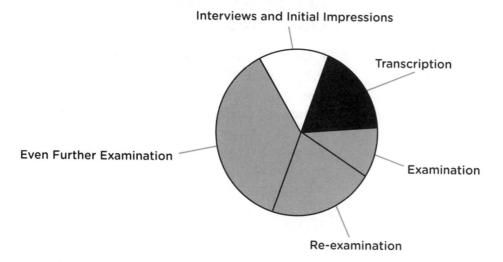

Interviews and Initial Impressions

Transcription

Examination

Re-examination

Even Further Examination

The Quantitative Method

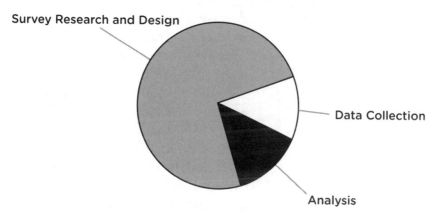

Survey Research and Design

Data Collection

Analysis

Alan Bucknam | Notchcode | 2011

Figure 4.8 portrays how the relative amounts of time and effort for different stages of research differs greatly between qualitative and quantitative methods.

What Are Some Examples of Methods Used by Other Students?

Mixed Methods Approaches

In an ongoing AR project, academics at the University Western Sydney and various stakeholders are working on risk communication and management associated with the Hawkesbury Water Recycling Scheme near Sydney, Australia. These researchers have found the most success with a mixed methods approach.

While working on an environmental management plan, they conducted a preliminary health risk assessment, which indicated a number of risk factors across the scheme. Also during this time, they identified *communities of practice* composed of people who were highly likely to come into contact with recycled water while performing their work duties. The researchers introduced the study to representatives from each community of practice and then set up discussions groups (focus groups). These discussions were used as a time for the group to talk about their concerns and their ideas about what might help address these particular concerns. The researchers documented the contents of each discussion group as qualitative evidence.

The researchers then decided to summarize the discussions by using simple causal loop diagrams. The researchers circulated the summaries and the diagrams to the communities of practice to ensure adequate representation. A workshop was held with representatives from each community of practice to discuss the diagrams and actions identified as next steps. The researchers then went forward with the actions approved by the group (Attwater & Derry, 2005).

The author made personal observations of individuals as well as groups, making sure to include all levels of staff in his observations as well as himself. He examined a variety of hospital documents, including financial reports, patient satisfaction records, staff satisfaction records, and documents on the hospital's process of care. In addition, the researcher did semistructured interviews with various levels of hospital staff. The researcher carefully documented all the issues that arose from his qualitative methods and systematically reviewed and analyzed them with hospital staff and executives. The researcher reviewed the quantitative data on a regular basis and worked to reconcile it with both personal observations and the perspectives of the staff.

Qualitative Approaches

In one AR project conducted at a hospital, the researcher used qualitative methods to get a general idea of the problems in the hospital according to the staff. The researcher interviewed all levels of staff to gather their opinions. Then, the researcher coded the responses for themes and found that many of the problems that the health care workers were having seemed to indicate issues in the hospital's culture. The researcher fed back the staff's own comments to them but in an organized manner revolving around different themes that the researcher had found. This

In a second study, based on a survey of hospital CEOs that found financial issues to be the most important problem facing their organizations (Erwin, 2009), one researcher decided to use AR to study the change process in a hospital. The hospital was trying to reduce costs while maintaining high-quality care for its patients. He used a variety of methods throughout his AR project, including both qualitative and quantitative.

researcher found that it was easiest to feed back the information using images, pictures, and cartoons that illustrated the themes or main problems with the hospital's culture.

The staff then took this data, and they came up with their own definitions for the very specific cultural issues they believed were at work in the hospital. The staff worked with the researcher to come up with a diagram to help them achieve the cultural change they all agreed was needed. On one side, they listed the negative aspects of the culture that they were hoping to get rid of, and then on the right side, they listed the attributes of the ideal culture they were trying to create. In this way, each negative item had a positive item that was to be the result of actions by staff. This proved helpful to staff when it came time to take action because they each had these visual reminders of what they were trying to move away from and what they were moving toward. This tool enabled the staff to constantly reflect on their actions and where they fell on the chart. The researcher also noted that this diagram was very useful in the evaluation process as they measured how far they had come in each area. The staff was able to look at the lists of words, document what actions they had taken, and judge the extent to which they had transformed the culture in each specific area (Bate, 2000).

In another study, a full-time employee of a dairy company decided to do some insider research to develop a food safety model in a business environment. This researcher used two different methods in the approach, focus groups and another group method called Nominal Group Technique (NGT). The focus groups were led by an independent facilitator, and each consisted of 12 consumers who were encouraged to share their views and concerns on issues of food safety and traceablity. The NGT consisted of a group of experts on food safety who had either academic knowledge or practical expertise. The format of the NGT was for a facilitator to ask a question and then go around the group in order, having each expert give his or her answer one at a time. The researcher analyzed the focus group comments to come up with a list of the most important food safety issues and concerns that were on the minds of consumers. Also, based on the consumer focus groups, the researcher developed a consumer typology that grouped consumers in to three main categories based on the types of answers they gave. The results of the NGT group were the development of a food safety model that took into consideration the three main consumer types. In this way, the food safety model was developed by experts but was driven by consumer feedback and had a focus on the main types of consumers (Doyle & Brannick, 2003).

What If I Can't Figure out How to Design the Data Collection and Analysis for My Research?

AR comes packaged with several almost automatic data sources. These include: reflective notes or journals, e-mails and other correspondence about the project, and comments from colleagues and classmates. Your particular project may also have some archival data that you can use. These records might include data from your human resource office, statistics from your local community, or census records. A researcher who is having difficulty designing may well find inspiration in filling in the following chart with what they do have, proposing ideas for the columns that aren't so obvious, and then discussing the whole with their colleagues and school professor.

The following chart is adapted from Maxwell (1996, p. 83). Researchers can employ these ideas to register both individual and group needs for data. This matrix is appropriate for qualitative, quantitative, or mixed data collection and gives you a place to plot analysis. We suggest that single researchers or PAR groups use this design process throughout multiple cycles of a project. Table 4.5, when implemented by you in your planning stage, will help define your needs for data.

Table 4.5 Planning Matrix for Data Collection and Analysis

What we need to know	Why we need to know it or action it pertains to	Data types and sources	Who and where	Timeline needed	Analysis

 ## Conclusion

Both qualitative and quantitative methods are used in AR and PAR projects. Each has their benefits and drawbacks depending on the specifics of the project. Some of the considerations in determining what methods to use are: time constraints, population size, availability of resources, areas of expertise, and the nature of what you are looking to accomplish. A good researcher needs to take into account the many facets of the situation and the intended outcome in order to make a good decision on which methods to employ. Often, researchers find that using mixed methods can be very rewarding and lead to the well-rounded and convincing evidence needed for further actions. Whatever methods you decide to choose, careful thought and planning must occur early on to ensure the greatest likelihood of success in your AR project.

Take Action

- Detail a timeline of activities that includes: researching the type of data collection and analysis you need, setting appointments and collecting data, carefully analyzing data, and reflective discussion with others prior to either your next cycle of research or final report.

- Start your reflective journal now, beginning with some thoughts on the methods you may want to use in your study. Carefully consider the amount of time and resources you might need to employ those methods to make sure your ideas are realistic. See Appendix D.

- Fill in the Planning Matrix (Table 4.5) to further narrow your ideas on what data you want to collect and how you will accomplish your goals.

- If you are ready, then narrow down what your first steps are for data collection and get started.

Additional Reading

Kock Jr., N. F., McQueen, R. J., & Corner, J. (1997). The nature of data, information and knowledge exchanges in business processes: implications for process improvement and organizational learning. *The Learning Organization, 4*(2), 70–80.

Chapter 5.
Working With People and Groups

Wicks and colleagues (2008) point to the importance of a "web of relationships, events, influences, role models and experiences which underpins action researcher's practice (and which has done so over time)" (p. 15). This chapter is meant as a reference throughout the AR or PAR process for issues relating to working with people and is written in the hopes that you will be able to use these premises to build a positive web and that through it you will have increased likelihood of sustainable results. The messages contained herein will hold true whether you are an action researcher working independently, as part of a team, or in a PAR group.

Working with people in the 21st century implies both face-to-face and virtual realities. International teams regularly use the methodology to advance situations in multinational corporations. There are AR projects implemented in MySpace, Facebook, and Second Life. The specifics of how to set up and work within live and virtual networks is covered in Chapter 6.

We mentioned the potential for failure in our first chapter as we discussed the work of Dorner (1996), and to quote from his book:

> Failure does not strike like a bolt from the blue; it develops gradually according to its own logic.

As we watch individuals attempt to solve problems, we will see that the complicated situations seem to elicit habits of thought that set failure in motion from the beginning. (p. 10)

To this, we might add that people working together influence each others' habits of thought and that it is critically important for people working together in research to build in important underlying structures for neutrality, analytical cohesive team interaction, and a positive outlook for the potential significance of their project. If and when AR or PAR projects fail, they most often do so because of issues that have to do with people, the groups or networks they work in, or power issues.

Yet, the literature is full of stories of people getting past significant power differentials to come out, after some work and dedication, to the long-term goal with sustainable new ways of working together. Most notable among these stories occurred in the 1980s between the huge multinational corporation Xerox, which partnered with the Amalgamated Clothing and Textile Workers Union (ACTWU). A quotation from their 1983 and 1986 contracts reads: "A Joint Company-Union Employee Involvement committee shall be established to investigate and pursue opportunities of enhancing employees work satisfaction and productivity" (Pace & Argona, 1991, 247). While a rocky road to implementation ensued, by 1988, reports showed millions of dollars of cost savings and productivity improvements.

Therefore, knowing that the stakes can be quite high, this chapter answers the following questions:

1. What skills do you need?

2. Are you an insider or outsider, and how does it matter?

3. What is the ideal model for a PAR group?

4. What does power have to do with it?

5. What if no one has time to work on the study?

6. In what way do ethics come in when working with groups?

7. What do PAR groups do?

8. What are some guidelines that groups can keep in mind in order to advance a PAR project?

9. What do you do when faced with defensiveness?

What Skills Do You Need?

We asked previous students what skills they used when working with people in their AR or PAR projects. Here is their list of skills with discussion. Throughout the chapter, we will also weave examples within the five topics.

- The ability to communicate

- The ability to uncover what motivates people

- The ability to uncover and move past both assumptions and defensiveness

- The ability to manage both your time and the project

- The ability to make effective decisions

The ability to communicate is important, in other words to listen and reframe in order to check your understanding. For instance, when your colleague or the person you are interviewing stops talking, you may say, "What I heard most from what you just said was . . .". This gives him or her an opportunity to correct any misperceptions you have and demonstrates the level of your attention.

The ability to uncover what motivates people was also mentioned by students. One student realized that "they are all motivated by different things. Some are motivated by additional opportunities, some are motivated by money, and some are simply not motivated to move beyond what they already know" (Laverty, 2010). How were these motivations uncovered—through active listening or through direct questions such as, "What do you find interesting or motivational in this situation?" or "What do you want to achieve?"

Also essential is the ability to uncover and move past both assumptions and defensiveness as they have the same root; a person is holding onto an idea as though it is the only course of behavior that is true or will work. Frequently, change is seen as a threat to power and authority, and this increases the likelihood of action researchers encountering defensive reactions both within themselves and from others. As practitioners have ideas about

Action Research for Business, Nonprofit, and Public Administration

which they feel strongly, the AR process enables them to unfreeze, surface, change, and rephrase their ideas or mental models. Adept practitioners understand that, during these moments when they believe the situation to be "wrong," they may be operating under the assumption that everyone shares their perceptions about the situation. Therefore, to call out multiple diverse perspectives related to an issue requires a certain skill in working with defensiveness, which we will go into in more depth later in the chapter.

The ability to manage both your time and the project are important skills that will impact your work with others. Partially, this has to do with planning ahead and then following through on what you say you're going to do when you say you're going to do it. Also, this has to do with being explicit so other people may easily work with you. PAR groups can meet ... and meet ... and meet ... and not move toward measurable action because they focus too long and too hard on what they discover. Finally, nothing takes away the impact of an AR project more than conflicting schedules diluting the attention of the key players on the project. Students often mention that competing time responsibilities between these projects and other course work is an

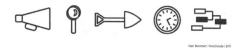

Alan Bucknam | Notchcode | 2015

In Figure 5.1 we see an illustration that demonstrates communicating, finding and uncovering motivations, managing your time and the project, and making effective decisions are key skills in working with groups.

issue, but whomever you work with will face these conflicts—discuss them and how you will work past them upfront.

The ability to make effective decisions is the final key. There are two parts to this; the first is time management. You need to be able to manage the time within the group setting and call for decisions to be made after sufficient time has been given to discussion; otherwise, PAR groups get stuck on one segment of the work and never move on to action. We look to Dorner (1996) for what makes a decision have long-term positive effects, and we find that it is the attention you give the decision after it has been put into action that helps with effectiveness. His findings were that, after a decision is made and some positive outcomes begin to appear, attention moves on prematurely to the next problem. All too often, the challenges that will naturally develop because of the first decision begin to assert themselves after that time, leaving a situation where no one is noticing the challenges until they become large and difficult to overcome.

Reflective Questions

- ✦ What experience do you have with the skills needed to manage groups?
- ✦ What is one time when you used these skills with other people and achieved a positive outcome?
- ✦ What is one time when you did not achieve a positive outcome, and what might you have done differently?
- ✦ What skills do you know you are lacking? Will you partner with someone who has them or develop them?

Are You an Insider or Outsider, and How Does It Matter?

Briefly referred to in an earlier chapter, insider research is that which is driven by someone employed by the organization he or she is studying. Increasingly, this can cause difficulties with IRB approvals. Assuming however, that permissions from both your university or the organization you are employed by or one you are working in as a consultant have been obtained, what positive attributes or challenges may develop as you work with people under these conditions?

Brannick and Coghlan (2007) focus on insider research through the viewpoint of three topics: access preunderstanding, role duality, and managing organizational politics, which are all useful for this discussion of the difference between insiders and outsiders. Insiders have access to information, history, and points of view that they have developed over the course of their employment while working within the organization under study. While it is true that some of that access may be limited by the same past history, there is much more to draw upon than would be available to a stranger. Likewise, they are likely to have firsthand understanding of the situation under study and what caused it. As with access, that can have a positive or negative effect dependent upon their ability to approach the topic without bias from a neutral stance. Two parts of this situation, role duality and the management of the organizational politics, may be more difficult for the insider. We discussed role duality in Chapter 2 under the ethics of a supervisor asking subordinates questions. In a similar fashion, a person at a lower level in the organization has difficulty asking hard questions of his or her superiors. They will also find difficulty in managing the organizational politics. All of these conditions require interpersonal skills that will need to be addressed during the course of the AR project. Bias and role duality may be linked as well, with people at lower or higher positions on a corporate scale of authority believing that they "know the truth" about the situation under study.

There can be ethical issues with supervisors asking questions of their subordinates. Conversely, employees at lower levels can have difficulty asking hard questions of their supervisors.

We refer our reader back to the discussion on the need for people using AR practice over a long period of time to develop both reflective and reflexive skills of reasoning. Several aspects of these styles of critical practice may come into play. For instance, researchers might consider having a question of whether and to what extent they or anyone participating in the study exhibited signs of bias as part of their weekly reflective protocol. Having it a regular question will raise it to a higher level of consciousness, increasing the likelihood that, during interactions, their reflexive awareness might pick up signs of subtle bias and allow them to either change their behavior or ask the other party to clarify. It is said that people at lower levels on a hierarchy have to learn to read the signs of those above them as a way to increase personal security. People at higher levels, however, may not have the same reflective and reflexive ability when addressing or interacting with those who play out more subservient roles. There are no cookie-cutter answers to these problems, and your research may or may not encounter them. If you do see some relevance with these issues, it is best to talk them through with your colleagues, professor, or supervisor as appropriate.

Greenwood and Levin (2007) suggest that "friendly outsiders" have skills they need as well. One very important skill is the ability to be able to reflect back to a group what they themselves say about what is going on, even those things that are unpopular or critical of certain people and situations, in such a way as to not create resistance. This is done through a balance of critique and support, ending feedback given in a variety of ways to different people

Action Research for Business, Nonprofit, and Public Administration

depending upon their roles in the organization. Accordingly, the friendly outsider must be able to get a wide range of people to open up and talk about both the positive and negative within their organizations, understanding that every perspective or role comes with its own likely viewpoints and barriers to accurate vision. The total of the vision of all these people, in all the roles throughout the organization, probably constitutes the best baseline understanding of what is going on. That does not mean that they will want to hear the perspective of the others they work with, and an action researcher will need to develop processes through which they may remain open to ideas they have not entertained before.

Outsider researchers come to the study with less likelihood of bias or potential for power struggles. Because they seem a neutral party, participants within the organization may open up more readily. Outsider researchers are also likely to bring new and varied perspectives with them, which may increase the potential for innovation. A consultant is an example of the friendly outsider role.

We believe in mixed-role groups to bring emancipatory change—that is our bias. To the extent that you can gather people who first and foremost care about your topic and then who also have various roles and authorities, you can make a group capable of getting something done. Stringer (1999), writing on CBPR, discusses the need for a "community profile" to be established as the baseline. This should include a discussion of the context, the players, the situations under which

Reflective Questions

- ◆ Have you decided whether you are doing your research as an insider or outsider?
- ◆ What benefits do you see as a result of your status as an insider or outsider to your study?
- ◆ What challenges may you face, and how do you see yourself moving past them?

they interact, significant historical features, and the issues or situations that lead to the current research. Clearly, this is easier for insider researchers or PAR groups for different reasons. Insider researchers have access to much of this information before they start. The PAR group has multiple access points and many people to collect information. However it is obtained, it is important that the researcher or team feed back to the larger community the overview or baseline information they have uncovered. The objective of this sharing of the baseline community profile is to check your preliminary understanding of the situation as you introduce yourself and your team as people who are capable of understanding and helping to create change.

What Is the Ideal Model for a Participatory Action Research Group?

It is ultimately up to you and your stakeholders what model for participatory research you choose to employ. As mentioned in Chapter 1, complete participation as equals of people who are not ordinarily at similar status can add democracy to a situation. Some situations or circumstances in business may not allow that, yet a team of people working together to complete an AR study will still be beneficial.

For instance, if you are in business, in what situations would you consider it helpful to have the voice of your best clients at the table? How about those other companies who are involved in your supply chain? See the References for an article by Coghlan and Coughlan (2006) on doing collaborative AR related to this situation. If you work in the nonprofit sector, what would be the situations in which you would want input from your clients? From your funders? If you work in public administration, when would you want representation from the current administration? From your clients or the public you serve? In all of these instances, what would their voices, as outsiders to your organization, add to your research or to your ability to address the issues you face?

Another question you may wish to ask is how or whether opening up your participatory group to your clients might be beneficial for them. Clearly, in nonprofit or public administration work, there would be instances where clients would find that working with professional staff could increase their self-efficacy and sense of empowerment. Freire and Freire's (1994) work demonstrated the ways in which AR can be self-empowering, ultimately changing the face of adult education in Brazil.

Students frequently ask many questions about the nuts and bolts of setting up their PAR teams. They ask, "How many people should there be, how should we choose them, how often should we meet, who should we include, and how should we begin?" Unfortunately, no one rule will be successful in all circumstances, but we can provide some general guidelines.

In determining how many people should be in your group, consider that solid group interaction is usually easier to maintain in groups from 6 to 12 people. How many people you invite depends on how long the project will be going on and how deeply it affects other people's lives. As an example, people are willing to commit to a short-term project more easily than they are to one that will likely be long term. If yours will last over a few months, you may need to invite twice as many people in order to ensure you have the support you need for the long haul.

The question of how often the group should meet is also one with variants in possibility. You have to meet often enough to keep the juice running between meetings. On the other hand, you can't meet so often that people burn out on the subject. In general, starting with a meeting every other week seems to be successful.

The question of who to include in your group will be based on many things, such as availability, interest, and dedication to the issue at hand. Because of the emancipatory potential of AR, groups are typically structured to contain as much diversity in personality, role, outlook, gender, ethnicity, cultural background, and age as possible. This solution is trickier at the beginning because you are calling together groups of people who are not used to working together, but over the long haul, they offer diverse opinions, and everyone learns more from each other than they would in a group that contained a lot of similarities. Trust will need to be built, but the outcomes can be worth the additional work at the beginning.

Once you have chosen a group and assigned meeting times, then you are ready to begin. One

Action Research for Business, Nonprofit, and
Public Administration

of our students reminded us, "When entering a project, organization of the team is critical. One must outline the structure of who is in charge and directing actions. Ensure everyone knows this so conflicting information received can be corrected quickly" (Keyser, 2010). This question of role definition within the team does not have to be static. Indeed, one of the most successful ideas in getting people to attend, work hard, and take ownership is to have rotating roles. For instance, a person facilitates for two meetings, while someone else scribes. That person then steps up to facilitate the next two meetings, choosing his or her scribe. However you decide to organize your team, it is good idea to agree upon the details of this organizational system in your first meeting.

Reflective Questions

- ✦ Who are you thinking of asking to participate in your team, and what do they each bring to the table?
- ✦ How are you going to go about deciding when and where to have your meetings?
- ✦ What are your ideas about the best way to organize your team?

What Does Power Have to Do With It?

The short answer to this question is, "Everything!" Power is at the root of both the successes and the failures of AR, and because power is only perceived in exchanges in the work and the relationship between people, we include it in this chapter. First, to look at the successes, AR is a democratic process built on the ideals of equality of voice and participation of all people in the process. As a result, it has a long history of emancipatory results, including the story in the previous chapter of the long-term coauthorship of a quality of life project at Xerox between two forces that would, in all other contexts, be at odds with one another—the company and the union.

AR, especially when mixed with the participatory ideal of including voices of the disenfranchised, can change whole sections of society by giving them the power to act. This was the case with the work of Paolo Freire when, in 1961 and 1962, groups of poor people (300 total) were taught to read and write in just 45 days because of his implementation of these ideals. The power issues that eventually led to his imprisonment came into play because, in Brazil, with literacy came the right to vote so that the ultimate outcome of his work was seen as disrupting to the new military regime. As Swantz (2008) reflects, "We have witnessed the potential of the research approach based on participation and communication. Together with breaking the monopoly of privileged knowledge also the monopoly of bureaucratic and technocratic power is broken" (p. 45). Gaventa and Cornwall (2008) remind us that, in addition to our conception of power as "power over," there is also power in linkages to others and that this power is fundamental in situations where activism is required and is "fundamental to transformational social change" (p. 175).

AR leads to increases in personal power as well. Knowledge is constructed through our interaction with the world and is therefore colored by our cultural contexts, our experiences, and the ways and types of knowledge formation to which we have been exposed. We construct it directly from exposure to resources, through our analysis of our actions, and through our reflections, thus improving our consciousness about the world around us (Gaventa & Cornwall, 2008). AR works in all three of these areas, which is why it is such an excellent professional development technique (Zuber-Skerrit, 1992). That leads us right back to power issues because increases in our knowledge, ability to act, and awareness or consciousness make us more powerful people.

Because it is true that AR projects lead to growth in power in a number of ways, it is wise to keep in mind that people currently in power are often adverse to signs of change that might endanger their positions in the world. Power struggles, therefore, are in one way or another likely to be the most frequent reason for failure in AR projects. People may be seen to use research to gain power over others or to advance their personal agendas. People in power sometimes try to squash AR success because they perceive it as a threat. In short, research and data gathering are never benign, and the person who is facilitating the process needs to be aware of that. These circumstances can be especially disappointing to the researcher who is doing the work with the goal of being entirely helpful, although they are, in fact, acting out of some very naive assumptions: (1) that all people want the same thing for each other, (2) that beneficence is a universal trait, (3) that people believe there is more than enough of whatever resources are being distributed and will choose to be generous, and (4) that people will help where they can. The beginning action researcher should ask him- or herself if any aspect of the work is based on any of those beliefs. When the answer is yes, extra sensitivity in the design may be needed.

Communication is the best weapon against a power struggle that would shut your project down or endanger your results from going further, but when people in power are not committed, you may have to realize you are facing a situation that will dampen if not override your results. From the beginning, it is generally good practice to understand the concerns of all your stakeholders and to report your activities and outcomes to them regularly in a manner that takes those concerns into account. On the positive side, you may convince the skeptic or stakeholder who has a fearful response to your activities that your work is going in a direction they can support, or you can enhance the natural support of other stakeholders, making it more difficult for a naysayer to have the level of impact needed to completely shut your work down. On the negative, you may find additional obstacles in your path.

Beware that some people who actually ask for work to be done may not support it at the end if it uncovers unexpected solutions. Do not let hidden messages go unchecked, and if you sense the beginnings of defensiveness on anyone's part, do what you can to diffuse it quickly. This returns us to the list of skills with which we started the chapter; uncovering what motivates people may allow you to spin the project in a manner that is seen as acceptable to the naysayers you face. Of course, situations may make this hard, such as when the person having difficulty with the project is one in authority, perhaps your boss. This is a reason that IRBs require written permission before allowing someone to take on research in a company, allowing the research to end

Action Research for Business, Nonprofit, and
Public Administration

before it even begins when the project does not find complete favor with the heads of the company.

Helpful Hints for Those Involved in Power Struggles

Remember, at its root, a power struggle is over a perceived shortage of something—which can range from money, benefits, and space to being given respect or being seen as "right." Assuming that you have gone the first step, to see the challenge through the eyes of the naysayer, there are a few facilitation techniques that may help:

Talking over issues in a group, building a list of possible solutions, use a grid or ladder to foresee outcomes, and voting on solutions can help avoid power struggles.

1. In a group setting, discuss the issues and formulate a cohesive picture of the problem.

2. Build a list of possible solutions, and be sure to include stopping the project as part of the list.

3. Build a grid or ladder, listing the solutions in such as way as the group can see the relation of both the steps that solution requires and the outcome it engenders. For instance, on the line that says "stop the project," list the activities involved (informing the community as an example) and outcomes that are involved in that step (disappointment of the participants).

4. Have everyone vote.

When possible, this strategy has several things that help it overcome a power struggle: First, the voting is public, so small-mindedness becomes public as well. This encourages better behavior by all participants. Second, everyone comes to understand what their

Reflective Questions

- ✦ What are your experiences with power struggles in the past, and how did you deal with them?
- ✦ What is the potential of your project in terms of equalizing power?
- ✦ What potential negative power issues exist?
- ✦ How do you plan to maximize the positive and minimize the negative potential?

ideas require and where they will lead, and as these are also discussed in a public forum, people understand each others' positions better as well. This helps people make better decisions. Third, it helps you as facilitator, because through it, you will come to understand the dynamics of the group. With the critical reflexive skills you have been building, this will lead to better potential outcomes in future debates.

What If No One Has Time to Work on the Study?

Faced with complex problems, people find themselves feeling as though they are running very hard just to keep up. This presents two specific issues that will need to be overcome by anyone charged with facilitating AR, making it hard to even sell the idea to do the project. There are two leverage points that may help. First, if faced with a complex situation, lots of time is currently being lost because of that problem. Therefore, any incremental move forward should pay off with releasing time or at least spending it on a solution rather than in the current frustrating manner that seems to have no end.

On the other hand, AR doesn't actually require very much outside time and can be easily folded into the daily routine once people understand the process. The discovery phase is probably the most time-consuming as it requires people to research information they do not already have. Split across multiple players, this won't add more than a few hours to each. Measurable actions will naturally be in line with work that is already ongoing, merely refining it and measuring the outcomes. The same is true with reflective protocol; it takes on average 15 minutes to half an hour a week and generates far more motivational energy and task orientation than it costs.

The key ingredient is to manage the ratio of extra work required with the benefits experienced so that everyone understands and sees the potential, which encourages them to support the work and the reasons for change. AR is a great process, and there will come a point where the work is self-motivating because the change has been much greater than anticipated, but you need to keep everyone working until you reach that point.

In What Ways Do Ethics Come in When Working With Groups?

There are several ways in which ethics can be compromised using AR. Issues include confidentiality, potentially undermining the work of others, ways and means of gathering data, sharing of data with others, and decisions about final reporting.

The requirement for group confidentiality systems varies widely depending upon the nature of the group and the relationship of the people in it, both professionally and personally. Client relationships need to remain confidential. That need must be discussed in any group as it begins and as frequently as necessary when the actions of particular persons are discussed within the group. Likewise, professional roles and authorities sometimes overlap or interweave. These distinctions should be discussed explicitly, and confidentiality procedures should be maintained. If your group is in public administration, then you may be subject to legislation that makes your documents open records. If this is the case, then you need to develop protocols for note-taking that maintain the confidentiality of persons whenever it is an issue. It is a good idea to discuss policies and procedures for confidentiality within the first meeting so that everyone is aware of and agrees to the rules of the group. It is also a good idea to keep an open discussion going throughout the AR project so that people can bring up any ethical issues they may feel need to be addressed.

Elliott (1991) discussed the dilemma of accidentally undermining a colleague because of data gathered during your study. How do you set boundaries in your discussions and interviews so that you set boundaries around your topic? As he put it, the dilemma "arises from a conflict between the value of critical openness and respect for the professional expertise of colleagues and their right to exercise authority within the confines of their roles within the organization" (p. 58). His work suggested two ways out of this dilemma: either to put boundaries on the discussions or to actively work toward building an organization-wide learning community where critical openness becomes the norm.

Critical openness may also come up against the ethical dilemma of who owns or controls various types of data. As an example, at the university of one of the authors, no AR passes the school IRB without a letter of permission from two role distinctions higher than the researcher within the organization under study. In nonprofit organizations, community members may feel they need to act as gatekeepers on community data in order to preserve the status quo. These same gatekeepers may also have informal if not formal rights of passing what will be included in a final report. CBPR in health care in rural settings often comes up against these issues, where inclusion of any small group of cases in a final report may interfere with the confidentiality of those persons due to the small size of the community as a whole. Sometimes, difficult decisions will need to be made in favor of either critical openness or community cohesion, depending on the circumstances.

What Do Participatory Action Research Groups Do?

PAR groups bring the potential of synchronicity to AR projects addressing large-scale issues. The purpose of any PAR group is to "engage in processes that enable people to work together productively" (Stringer, 2007). There are five basic things that PAR groups do: ferret out information, test their initial ideas against broadly held beliefs within the communities they serve, design and implement several small steps aimed at improving the situation under study, reflect individually and as a group, and report back on findings.

Ferret Out Ideas

For large-scale projects, the best way to start a PAR group is to hold preliminary meetings of small groups of similar stakeholders in places in which

Reflective Questions

✦ What are some of the key ethical issues that you are concerned about in your project?

✦ What are some of the issues surrounding confidentiality that you will need to deal with?

✦ What is your plan for addressing ethical and confidentiality issues with your group?

they are comfortable, as opposed to large community spaces such as schools and universities. The purpose of this preliminary meeting is to gather information from people whose voices are not usually heard on the current circumstances. Once people have attended a smaller meeting, they can be encouraged to elect a spokesperson and have that person speak for them during the rest of the PAR group meetings.

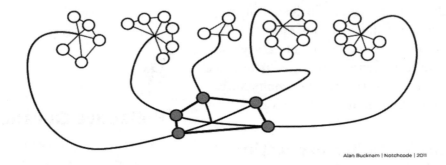

Alan Bucknam | Notchcode | 2011

Figure 5.2 illustrates that small stakeholder groups allow voices that aren't usually heard to speak up; spokespeople from each group can then gather together to represent those voices at later PAR group meetings.

Test Ideas

It isn't enough to think you know what is entailed in the situation; that knowledge has to be tested. Again, groups can do this easily and in a number of ways from going back to their original sources with the conglomerate view and testing out its viability to employing a small-scale community survey with each PAR member responsible to collect data.

Implement New Solutions

When the baseline of ideas is consistently agreed upon, it is time to start strategic planning. Often in one group meeting, participants can develop a

Action Research for Business, Nonprofit, and Public Administration

series of potential activities and put them in logical progressive order with an agreed-upon timetable for implementation. Group process is handy here too, as groups of people have more resources to draw upon than most individuals, increasing the likelihood of large projects having the support they need.

Reflect on Lessons Learned

One of the beauties of the AR and PAR process, as we have mentioned before, lies in the fact that they require reflection. We recommend, at the end of one meeting, the facilitator points out that the next meeting will require a reflective process and that they encourage everyone to individually reflect in the time between meetings. To the extent that this happens, the group reflection is enriched.

Report Back

It is important that our communities have access to the legacy of our ideas and our work. There are many ways that this information can be distributed. If your project only affects your company, nonprofit, or office, then reports can be left out in common areas or relevant locations as reading material for your colleagues. If your public administration office is working in a neighborhood, a notice on what your group is doing can be posted in a library on a bulletin board. In urban environments, you may want to post on community Internet sites or as a press release. Finally, in networks that are separated by large geographic distances or for issues that affect a wide number of people, consider posting a video or slide report on the Internet. Chapter 7 will cover how to analyze data and write the best report for your stakeholders.

Reflective Questions

- How will you gather the initial data for your project?
- What level of community reporting are you considering throughout your project?
- What expertise will each participant or team member provide?

What Are Some Guidelines That Groups Can Keep in Mind in Order to Advance a Participatory Action Research Project?

Basic guidelines for the commitment you ask for from your group members include the following:

1. Agree upon a series of meeting dates with the commitment to attend.

2. Show respect for all group members by arriving on time and listening carefully when someone is speaking.

3. Allow for good facilitation so that no one speaks more than their turn and that meetings follow a structured agenda.

4. Make a focused commitment over that period of time to making a difference on the issue under study, bringing all thoughts and activities related to this study to each meeting for discussion.

5. Maintain confidentiality about the substance of group discussions outside of the group as well as following all ethical guidelines set forth by the group.

Remember that managing not only research but change requires many steps. First, watch closely for the results of your actions and then, over time, recraft your project as subtleties emerge and evolve into greater understanding of the issues you face (James, 2009). Dorner's (1996) research on failure focused on teams of people trying to improve the lives of others in complex situations. When all the teams were consistently unsuccessful in their task, he measured the differences between teams and their levels of outcomes. Some participants within those teams displayed more skills than others; these he dubbed the "good" participants. We can learn a lot by looking at their characteristics.

Here are the characteristics of good participants, according to Dorner (1996), and their benefits:

1. They made more decisions, and there were shorter time periods between the decisions they made. From making lots of decisions in quick periods of time, we see an example of flexibility and a watchful eye on results. For example, if something starts to change in a way that is not desired, the person has enough flexibility and time to effectively reverse or amend his or her original decision.

2. They focused on not only primary goals in the decisions they made but also on their secondary effects. By creating a focus on not just the one goal but all of its secondary effects, the action researcher displays an ability to be holistic and is thus less likely to run into a mess of his or her own creation later.

3. They designed their decisions with the whole complex system in mind. Some people have more innate ability to see the complex whole than others, but what we don't have in nature, we can borrow with good advisers, who we can

assign to keep us up on how the whole system is responding to change.

4. They were able to discern the underlying larger issues and start to make decisions there. In a similar fashion, some people naturally discern a large, underlying truth that propels a system in a certain direction, but once again, it is not necessarily natural and can be brought in through a team member.

5. They tested what they wanted to do in a small way before implementing a big change. Researchers frequently rely upon pilot studies to test early hypotheses; the same can be said in the measurable action sequence for action researchers. This was brought up in the first section of this chapter when we mentioned that time management is often closely related to focusing on the project.

6. They asked why and probed for underlying causality. As mentioned in Chapter 4, probing the underlying motivations of the people involved in your study draws you into deeper levels of reflective wisdom, increasing the likelihood for a breakthrough in understanding.

7. They were not easily distracted; they responded rather than reacted. Distraction by people in charge of making decisions occurs when they have more responsibilities than they can manage on their own. In any group working together, one or a number of people can be assigned the task of watching carefully for both desirable and undesirable outcomes.

8. They were slightly more innovative in their decisions than following in historically stable patterns. Finally, in a situation that demands change, the ability to embrace innovation seems a natural requirement.

Finally, Gustavsen, Hansson, and Qvale (2008) remind us that there is more in the use of AR to lead change within an organization than just keeping close track of things, as in Dorner's (1996) list. They would add to our list of important things to keep in mind the requirement of making note of dialogue and communication as they occur, which when used as data, make note of growth relationships. Beyond that, there is leadership and trust. Using data and capturing growth allows the people working together to celebrate their success. Successful joint-action engenders trust between participants, which in turn, leads to greater readiness to engage with others in the next cycle of change.

What Do You Do When Faced With Defensiveness?

People may feel they need to protect themselves from change, and because a well-run AR or PAR project will undoubtedly result in change, running up against defensiveness is not unusual—from both your participants and from the wider community that may be affected. As Argyris (1990, 2002b) taught us, defensive reactions of the "don't shoot the messenger" variety can have extreme deleterious effects. For example,

Reflective Questions

✦ What guidelines for commitment will you present to your potential group members?

✦ How will you ensure that all members follow the guidelines?

✦ Which of Dorner's (1996) suggestions have the most relevance to your project?

to what extent in business would your company support the publication of information that held the company in a bad light? In the nonprofit sector, could your final data show ways in which the organization was not meeting its mission? Or could you publish information that might be construed as negative on the part of your clients? As public servants, could your final report suggest deficiencies in the current administration? Could you discuss laws that were not being upheld or federal funds that were not correctly allocated? All of these may occur as outcomes in AR projects.

To answer the question of what to do when faced with defensive interactions while facilitating an AR project, we draw on the work of Argyris, Putnam, and Smith (1985) in their treatise on action science. They suggest a method of creating action in situations where things are stuck by confronting that which does not want to move. The skill of confronting has three steps: pointing out, inquiring into, and then analyzing the consequences of living out of the assumptive or defensive posture. Argyris and Schön (1974) and later Senge (1994) expanded the work with defensive behavior and created what they called the **ladder of inference** (see Figure 5.3). This problem-solving strategy for systems thinking can be used to help understand the development of inference. Both assumptions and defensive behaviors rest on a foundation of a person inferring truth from his or her personal experience.

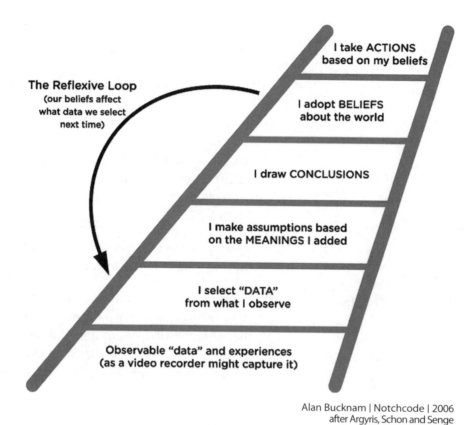

The Reflexive Loop
(our beliefs affect
what data we select
next time)

I take ACTIONS
based on my beliefs

I adopt BELIEFS
about the world

I draw CONCLUSIONS

I make assumptions based
on the MEANINGS I added

I select "DATA"
from what I observe

Observable "data" and experiences
(as a video recorder might capture it)

Alan Bucknam | Notchcode | 2006
after Argyris, Schon and Senge

Figure 5.3: Ladder of Inference

Let's assume your company, nonprofit, or public administration office has a new manager who has been brought in to balance the budget. If you heard this person talking and the only phrase you heard was "changes that need to be made around here," what would you infer? How would you feel? Many times, employees jump to assume that their jobs might be at risk or that a change might negatively affect them, and then they begin to behave as though that the assumption is true even before the change had been implemented.

So, how might you use this tool in your circumstances:

1. Take notes at the next meeting with a wide side column laid out on your sheet. Whenever something occurs in the meeting that triggers defensiveness in the group, make note of it in that column.

2. Later, point out to the group the sections around which you noticed defensiveness and invite them to inquire into it with you.

3. Show them the ladder of inference and ask someone to walk through the steps—what did they observe, what assumptions did they make, and what conclusions did they draw? Discuss differences among people in the group on that set of steps.

4. Discuss as a group what the consequences are of this defensiveness. Brainstorm other possibilities that might ensure greater longevity to the group and the project.

In most cases, this direct confrontation and levelheaded discussion ease the tension in that defensive parties can consider other postures.

Reflective Questions

+ What is your experience in dealing with defensive reactions from others?
+ When have you had a defensive reaction to something?
+ How will you deal with your own potential defensiveness in this project?
+ What are some ways you might use the ladder of inference?

Conclusion

Working with people can be very rewarding but also has its challenges. There are certain skills that will be very useful to you in your AR project when you will inevitably end up working with others. We have compiled some of the top skills reported by other students as helpful along with ways that you may be able to work on improving these skills. If you decide to do your research as an insider or an outsider, you should be aware of the specific issues that may arise as you work with others within a particular organization. There are pros and cons to working with others on an AR project in your own place of employment versus an organization that you have less experience with. It is important to be aware of the interpersonal dynamics and how they may differ as an insider versus an outsider.

Setting up a good PAR team does not have set rules, but there are general guidelines. Using information in this chapter, you should have ideas that will help you start to consider who to include in your group, how many people, when and where to meet, and even how to begin your first meeting. You will need to pay careful attention to ethical and confidentiality issues within your group throughout your project. You will also need to come up with guidelines about how the group will behave ethically, make decisions, and generally interact with one another. It is a good idea to cover many of these important topics when your team first meets. Also, in this chapter, we covered what it is that a PAR team actually does. This should give you a good outline to follow as you progress through your project. As you conduct your AR project, you will undoubtedly encounter defensiveness from others and maybe even yourself. The ladder of inference may be a helpful tool in dealing with the issues inherent in defensive interactions that may occur throughout your project.

It will be very important for you to remember the lessons from power differentials: Ethical issues may arise in work situations where some have more authority and power than others, stakeholders may use power to influence your project, and withholding information can lead to sabotage. When successful, your project may be **emancipatory research** or what Swantz (2008) refers to as "breaking the monopoly of privileged information" (p. 45), which leads us to our favorite quote from Margaret Mead: "Never doubt that a small group of thoughtful, committed citizens can change the world. Indeed, it is the only thing that ever has."

 ## Take Action

Begin drafting a list of people you may want to include in your project in one capacity or another. Make sure to note what benefits they may bring to the group, including areas of expertise and resources, as well as any drawbacks to having them included on the project. You can also start to think about when and where you might like to have your first meetings.

Draft a document with key issues that you will need to address with your team. You will want to decide how you are going to come up with the guidelines for the group. Will you make the guidelines and then present them to the group, or will making the guidelines be a group process? You should be able to have a good outline of the key issues that you need to deal with in your first team meeting.

Additional Readings

Downey, L. H., Ireson, C. L., & Scutchfield, F. D. (2009). The use of photovoice as a method of facilitative deliberation. *Health Promotion Practice, 10*(3), 419–427.

Hearn, G., Foth, M., & Gray, H. (2009). Applications and implementations of new media in corporate communications. *Corporate Communications: An International Journal, 14*(1), 49–61.

Inglegard, A., Roth, J., Shani, A., & Styhre, A. (2002). Dynamic learning capability and actionable knowledge creation. *The Learning Organization, 9*(2), 65–77.

Lee, C. W. (2007). Is there a place for private conversation in public dialogue? Comparing stakeholder assessments of informal communication in collaborative regional planning, *American Journal of Sociology, 113,* 41–96.

Mosher, H. (2009). Issues of power in collaborative research with dignity village. *Cultural Studies <=> Critical Methodologies, 10*(1), 43–50.

Themudo, N. S. (2009). Gender and the nonprofit sector. *Nonprofit and Voluntary Sector Quarter, 38*(4), 663–683.

Chapter 6.
Networks and How to Employ Them for Change

It is important to discuss the practical consider-ations involved in embedding PAR in network environments and other forms of communities of practice because more and more business is now conducted in networks. NPAR can be seen as a significant tool for creating long-term systemic change in a complex environment. Why? Because of the power of the group to ferment activity over time and because many hands make light work. As this book presents tools and techniques in AR to help develop sustainable change in complex situa-tions, we address how to run an AR project across a diverse network.

What is a network? For our purposes, a network is defined as a group of people connected to one another either in a face-to-face situation or aided by some type of technology. The people in the network may or may not know each other or have any under-standing about each other's strengths or weaknesses.

Before we begin, let us consider for a moment the similarities and differences between employing AR in a network or in a large-scale environment. Martin (2008) discusses two examples of large-scale change: one for a school board association affecting 40,000 students, the other a community facing poor relations among its diverse population. The three considerations that she brings to the fore would equally hold true in the networked situations in which we have worked:

1. Before starting the project, it is important to ask which subpopulations are currently not given voices and to ensure that they are included. In a large group, these are often those who have met with disparaging comments in the past and so choose to stay habitually quiet. In a network, these are often the newcomers to the group.

2. The participatory idea of coresearchers breaks down exponentially with the increase in the number of stakeholders. Both large-scale and networked AR has this difficulty. This is the reason we have found success in the **hub and spoke** approach outlined in this chapter.

3. The larger the project, the more difficult it is to manage the communication flow so that the greatest number of people have the ability to learn from measurable actions taking place in other areas. Networks, on the other hand, often pass off information from connectors to their small group of interested parties. The hub and spoke design used in both large-scale projects and networks increases the chances that information may reach everyone. We agree with this author that it is a lot of work—one that demands a team of people facilitating the project.

4. The requirement of the project to include the widest range of voices, when employed

in a large-scale environment, means that the facilitators will need to build flexibility into their design. This is true as well for networks because the population of stakeholders will ebb and flow with the participants, creating new challenges to capture all the voices.

The business community's understanding of the potential for communication and growth by establishing networks continues to grow in importance. Our experience has validated the use of rolling out an AR study over a diverse geographic area through a network of online communication. We therefore recommend that leaders employ a hub and spoke NPAR design whenever they want to implement a complex reform.

This chapter addresses these questions:

- Why use NPAR?

- What are networks, and how are their attributes in line with AR?

- What is the hub and spoke PAR design?

- What are the necessary ingredients for a successful networked AR project?

- How is the hub and spoke PAR design employed for dynamic change or reform?

- How do people connect in a networked design?

- Does a network have to preexist, or can you start one for the project?

- Are there examples of NPAR?

- How could virtual tools, learning management systems, or social networking platforms be used to your network's advantage?

Why Use Networked Participatory Action Research?

The world is changing faster than systems can keep up. This is seen in business, industry, education, health care, banking, and so on. These stressors are changing the world of nongovernment organizations (NGOs), nonprofits, and public administration as all the services are straining to keep up. Directors, owners, and managers believe they see where the organization needs to move but have difficulty explaining or motivating current staff to make the necessary changes. **Networked participatory action research (NPAR)** will focus the energy of a group on creating sustainable solutions to these problems.

These are not small issues. Sometimes, the issues are embedded within cultural change as in a merger situation. While in much of the world, the government or multinational corporations have always been the best employers, now economic pressures are moving populations toward a change to an entrepreneurial society. Huge shifts need to occur to create economic growth in the new knowledge-based economic environment, and no one has all the answers or knows exactly how to lead the process. Using these examples, we see that you and organizations you work for may face any one of the following complex situations:

- Producing a shift in motivation in your staff or community so that people work together differently and more efficiently face issues collaboratively.

- Encouraging a shift from seeking only safety to being willing to take risks.

- Needing to incorporate the soft skills of teamwork and collaboration that are required in modern business.

- Providing professional development for staff so that they can model these new skills, ones that they don't currently have or understand.

- Finding the time to release all the staff for this training and this retooling while still continuing the work that needs to be accomplished.

- Finding a way for the change to be embraced by the people rather than engendering resentment.

As is true with most complex matters, facing these issues directly makes many experienced leaders and managers hesitate because of the likelihood of potential failure. We have all seen reform efforts gone bad. Every new idea that does not get implemented properly leaves behind it a residue of resentment and skepticism, eventually souring the entire culture of our working world. Many Western environments

Finding time to allow staff to train and accomplish normal work tasks is one issue faced by organizations tackling systemic change.

have seen this already, with employee morale dropping dramatically and productivity coming to a halt upon announcement of mergers, reorganization, and so on.

The good news is that NPAR can overcome many, if not all, of these challenges. This section lays out the general format that can be used by leadership, in tandem with a good PAR facilitation, to develop teams of staff who will study the issues and develop solutions, taking ownership of the changes required by the complex situation rather than subtly opposing all change. Because they engage with current theory and research as they study the issues in their local context, PAR researchers create fast-paced personal development resulting in greater leadership at all levels (James, 2007; National College for School Leadership, 2006; Zuber-Skerrit, 2011).

What Are Networks and How Are Their Attributes Useful in Action Research?

A network refers to a group of people connected to one another, either in a face-to-face situation or aided by some type of technology. The people in the network may or may not know each other or have any understanding about each others' strengths or weaknesses. This is common in facilitating a PAR team as well, that the facilitator may or may not know the people and they may or may not know each other. In that sense, doing AR across a network

Reflective Questions

- ✦ What situations in your life might benefit from NPAR?
- ✦ What theory and research might such a team benefit from studying?
- ✦ Who would need to take ownership in order to have the project move forward?

is not all that much more difficult than calling together a small group in the local community.

Creativity in Groups

The first desirable attribute of networks is that much creative activity happens in groups when people get a chance to play off of each other (Barabasi, 2002, 2005, Sawyer, 2007). It is with the intention of harnessing that creativity toward a desired outcome that will lead an organization to employ NPAR. It is participating in a creative environment that will motivate the participants to engage fully and create change.

An example of a network focused on creativity and innovation is a group of 70 university teachers from Spain who have developed a network on innovation and formative assessment in higher education, operating since 2005. Their basic methodology of work has been AR where they report very positive results in different aspects in improving their educational practices, generating a network, sharing experiences across new linkages, and enhancing the learning of their adult students. They have wrapped issues of innovation and creativity throughout their work through their research and into their practice (Pastor, 2010).

Interconnectedness and Transparency

Most of the attributes of networks have to do with communication. There is a familiar saying related to the connectedness of the world, "It's a small world." This phenomenon is a common attribute of networks, the appearance that we are all linked through a short path of connectedness to each other across networks (Siemens, 2009). One of our authors lives in Ireland, and there, the first conversation that people have is where they are from and who they know in common. In the United States, where it is more likely that people come from diverse physical locations, the first topic of conversation is, "What do you do?" Both of these very different topics have the same end result, raising to awareness mutual networked connections. In Ireland, connections are built on having known someone in childhood or being related; in the United States, they are built on mutual awareness of each others' work—both conversations are seeking out whether this new person is part of a preestablished network of relations.

Because of the interconnectedness of the different parties in the network, secrets are hard to keep. Said another way, networks encourage transparent activity. This can play havoc with confidentiality issues if not addressed directly by the action researcher.

As an example, in a study in Denmark, a group of researchers at a diabetes center are building new, large alliances, taking in whole municipal settings and investigating how they can make sustainable changes in health care from a positive, participative perspective. The researchers look at how change can be promoted, and the practitioners work on what to change. This multiprofessional approach requires interconnectedness and as much transparency as can be managed by all parties because they come to the work from different contexts and theoretical understandings and with practical ideas of what is involved in the work.

What confidentiality issues might arise? Because the researchers are from two different organizations, their administrations might be concerned that others would understand and form opinions about their operations. Trust must be formed: trust from the participants that the researchers won't tell tales about the challenges they are facing and trust from the researchers that they don't have to guard their words because the participants understand that they are trying to help.

Let's take another case. A large mentoring organization is having difficulty recruiting African American male mentors. An outsider researcher student comes to them wanting to help. They have to trust her with their statistics (how many youth have been waiting how long) so that she will be well armed to advocate for them with African American groups such as 100 Black Men. In turn, she has to trust the agency staff to tell her the whole story. The student needs to feel secure that her reputation stays strong with the organizations in her network with whom she advocates.

In either of these cases, what would work if the trust was not forthcoming or if any party began to feel less than comfortable? The answer lies in more transparency, having the courage to come to a meeting and discuss your lack of ease as an important step to rebuilding trust. Hopefully, the other party will respond in kind. If not, then it is up to you to reevaluate your position in the network and in the AR project.

Hubs

The third attribute of networks is the transfer of information through hubs of activity. Airlines may choose a city to be a hub, a home base for interactivity as their passengers transfer to planes going to different locations. Information in a network may travel in a similar pattern, starting with one group or small cluster but quickly transferring through a hub, where more activity is generated, and then spreading quickly across the wider network. An example of this would be that, when people in the hub of AR activity share ideas, they take these ideas into their businesses or schools where they are dispersed. Staff in those locations may take the idea on to their networks as well, causing a chain of events. Hubs give people who are closely connected to the center of activity a disproportionate amount of apparent power because they hear (and can implement) the new ideas first.

An example of the hub and spoke design (to be discussed later in the chapter) is our own online network that covered a total of 45 geographic locations over a 6-year period of time. Supporting local teams of principals of schools, teachers, and community members, hubs of activity brought the diverse groups together on a bimonthly basis for discussion. Local teams worked together on AR and PAR projects in between times, advancing educational opportunities for their students experiencing homelessness (James, 2006a, 2009).

The Power of Weak Ties

Finally, because relationships across networks are based on a single aspect of our lives, it would be rare that they would develop the close connection of friends and family. It is this **weak tie** or connection that gives them their power to change understanding or lives (Granovetter, 1995; Granovetter & Swedberg, 2011). Think of the last time you looked for work—while family and friends can offer solace, it would be those in your professional network who would be more likely to have ideas that you would want to pursue. This idea of weak ties becomes important in networks when you consider how data are transferred. On the one hand, groups may have access to a far wider range of information than they originally realize when they put questions out through their networks. On the other hand, information gathered (or rather hinted at) from diverse sources may be much harder to track down. Figure 6.1 illustrates that loose social networks can spread ideas through weak ties between more close-knit communities.

An example of how information can come to us through our AR network that can make a major change in our project or work on the issues we face comes from a networked project in the UK in which a group of schools committed to come together as a network. Each school committed to establishing a group of practitioner researchers; these varied in size, some groups including just a couple of people, whilst others involved all staff in the school. Through the activities of this network, these representatives from member schools met each other on regular occasions at planned events. To begin with, the exchanges between action researchers from differing organizations were concerned with the specific details of the projects being conducted within each school and were limited to the events that had been planned. But over time, relationships developed, and the groups of collaborating action researchers began to include people from different schools. As these groups started to change, so the nature of communication also developed.

Action researchers have always shared their interests about the development of their practice, for example, in exploring how best to involve pupils in planning their own learning activities. Over time, they increasingly began to share in the process of AR as well, for example, comparing and sharing approaches to evidence gathering or ways to relate the AR groups to others in the school. But, these action researchers also became the conduits for the interest of their colleagues as well. Their intimate knowledge of the other staff in their own school meant that, through conversations with other action researchers, opportunities arose for establishing contact between people whose interests, expertise, and concerns coincided but who were not themselves active participants in the network itself.

Using the ties metaphor, the core group of action researchers gained benefit from establishing closer ties with each other, ties that had not necessarily previously existed, but in doing so, the other staff which whom they had contact were linked through an extended network of loose ties because of their relationships with network activists without ever having

Reflective Questions

✦ According to the definition of networks presented above, what are your experiences of working with people in a network?

✦ Which of these attributes was most important or memorable in your experiences of working within networks? Why?

to actively engage in network activities themselves. For more information on the operation of networks of this nature, see Day and Hadfield, 2004, and Day and Townsend, 2007, 2009. Figure 6.1 illustrates how we never know which ideas may influence the communication among and between groups.

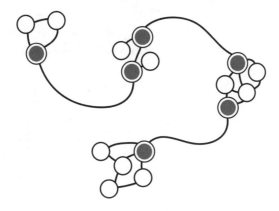

Ideas propagate through networks via **weak ties.**

Alan Bucknam | Notchcode | 2011

Figure 6.1 illustrates that loose social networks can spread ideas through weak ties between more close-knit communities.

What Is the Hub and Spoke Participatory Action Research Design?

Hub and Spoke Design

Picture a central hub with smaller circles attached to it by lines and then more lines making a web between the smaller circles. That is our preferred design of NPAR to address complex change.

First, small working groups are formed in each of the hubs of activity that need to address the change. For instance, in international business, you would bring together working teams that include directors of units in different locations where the change needs to be implemented. The directors would bring key players from the organization to meet with the larger group (the hub) and then leave and implement an AR cycle in their local settings. Why is this design the one we recommend? Because the communication pattern among different hubs can be managed easily. The local teams agree to a protocol for communication, and the meetings in the hubs catch up groups that may have

The Hub and Spoke Model

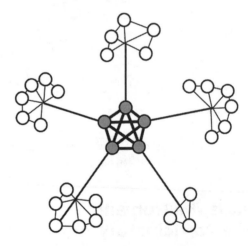

Alan Bucknam | Notchcode | 2011

Figure 6.2 shows a hub and spoke design, illustrating representatives of each small team coming together to interact at the spoke while allowing for communication of small-group concerns and progress across the entire network through the hub.

Action Research for Business, Nonprofit, and Public Administration

fallen behind. This helps the facilitator of the project to stay on top of the ongoing activities and to coordinate efforts to ensure valid and reliable results.

Once these small teams are formed (becoming the smaller outside circles in our diagram at the ends of the spokes), you bring them together into the hub on a regular basis to facilitate their understanding of AR, their understanding of the challenges the wider organization faces, and what is expected of their individual subgroups. Then, the teams go back to their areas and proceed with a cycle of AR. This includes discovering what is currently in the way of the change and measuring it. Then, they come back to the hub for another day's work, where a facilitator guides the formation of next steps, which includes designing and planning the implementation that will begin to create the change desired. Because participants are held to a standard that requires later reporting, each step along the way is measured, and as the process continues, they grow in their professional understanding of this scientific approach to problem solving and change.

A Timetable for Implementation

The timetable starts with management assigning the work to their managers and the managers choosing their teams. Then, these teams or hubs of activity come together with the facilitator to learn about AR and to plan the rest of the change effort. If this were a dissertation or thesis or if time permitted, they could gather for a year in face-to-face meetings or for a web conference every 2 months. The structure stays the same, but the length of time between meetings shortens or lengthens depending on the needs of the situation. In total, including initial planning and final celebration, the facilitated group meets for a total of 8 to 10 working days, spaced evenly through the amount of time available.

The teams will put in about three times that much effort in their local contexts. We have studied groups using this design and have found consistently transformational results—both from the teams in the hubs of activity and in the organization as a whole. Generally, 8 to 10 sessions of facilitated activity and twice that to disseminate what they have learned will engender change in local environments that demonstrate remarkable differences. The following quotes from participants at the end of this design demonstrate the results you might expect in an organization.

> The cycles of participatory action research have certainly given us exciting results. Motivation in our organization is an ongoing research topic, and we realize that we have a duty to pass on this information to the entire community. We all need to raise our expectations as to our ability to achieve better results, but we have proven to ourselves that we are up to the task. (Morfitt & Cox, 2008)

> The action research process has pushed all of us to continue to refine our practice of acquiring usable information. As we went through this cyclical process, we gained clarity on the data needed to be most helpful to those we work with and our employers. Everyone assisted by seeking information and we created an environment where all were successful. The process supported us and caused us to grow beyond our wildest dreams. While at time frustrating, it also creates an effective model for successful implementation of change. (Cook, Heintzman, & McVicker, 2004)

What Are the Necessary Ingredients for a Successful Networked Action Research Project?

The first ingredients that must be in place for a successful networked project include: a knowledgeable consultant or facilitator, extrinsic motivation to do the work, all the supports necessary in place from the parent organization, and a commitment by all to let the process run for a given period of time. The facilitator needs to be skilled at understanding the process as a whole and have experience managing projects and groups. We have found stipends given to participants who finish the project and write final supports to work best as outside extrinsic motivators. Resources from the sponsoring organization in terms of time and commitment of rooms or other resources send the message that the work is important so participants take it seriously.

Networked activity, if not carefully coordinated in terms of its focus and outcome, can result in different hubs of activity that involve diverse approaches to the topic. This lack of cohesion can render the data collected in the project meaningless. Validity and reliability of the measurable data require that collection and analysis are performed in the same manner in multiple locations. This is a coordination challenge, and the network needs to address this issue from the beginning.

Lastly, the network needs to set up protocols for reflective and reflexive discussion on a regular basis.

Facilitators organize meetings, take and distribute notes, and keep communication flowing between meetings.

We recommend an immediate institution of weekly or biweekly reports filled out by all participants and sent to the facilitator as the first step in active accountability. Then, by using the information coming in from these reports (anonymously of course), during the next meeting's discussion, the group will be well on its way to establishing the trust and transparency needed to focus reflexively on their own individual and group processes and norms. It is important to model for others an ability to be nondefensive in the face of criticism. Then, we can begin to see how that affects future transparency in the group.

When a parent organization desires to run a successful networked project for longer than 6 months to a year, we recommend a selection of people to be trained as in-house facilitators. During the first few cycles of researcher, they learn how to facilitate the work and act as the eyes and ears for the consultant in between meetings. At the end of that time, they take over the project.

What Is the Facilitator's Role?

To fulfill the first major requirement, someone has to take the role of facilitator and to take on the responsibility of organizing regular meetings, taking notes, distributing them, and maintaining communication between meetings. Generally, the facilitator is a student who is working for university requirements or a consultant who has experience in managing this process in diverse situations. This facilitator ensures that two major criteria are met so that the PAR project can work successfully using networks. First, there needs to be a way for the people on the network to meet regularly and communicate as they go through the AR process. Second, everyone needs to agree to follow the established processes as they go through the project.

While the hub and spoke design has proven to be successful, other networks may require variations on that theme. The student or consultant facilitator needs to thoroughly understand the natural characteristics of the network and then to flexibly set up regular meetings to facilitate the PAR process. This may require use of virtual tools or a blend between face-to-face meetings and meetings in online spaces. In order to ensure success, communication must be well documented.

What Support Is Needed From the Parent Organization?

We have found that certain concrete levels of support from the parent organization greatly enhance the likelihood of absolute success in encouraging positive outcomes in complex situations.

1. Eight to twelve people, offices, or departments chosen as good potential sites to come into the hub for meetings to work on the changes envisioned. Participants from those sites should be the director or lead manager and two or more of their staff, who are chosen to make up the local teams (the spokes).

2. Support for a stipend to be given to all participants when they complete their final reports. We have seen this amount be anywhere from

Reflective Questions

+ How are your teams going to meet regularly and communicate?
+ How will you use face-to-face meetings and virtual tools?

$750 to $3,000 a person but have come to believe that companies also need to be able to rely on the participants' self-interest in the project as well as a natural desire to do a better job.

3. Support for 8 days of meeting times with the six to eight local teams meeting with the facilitator, their assistants, and the people chosen to become facilitators the next year.

4. Support for the consultants in terms of providing local assistants—these people serve to help set up the meetings and as local support systems.

5. If the project is to last beyond a year, then support for two additional half days of work surrounding each meeting is needed, one before and one after the 8 days described above. This is for the eight people chosen to learn facilitation and take over the project in future years. Before the hub meeting, they debrief what they have seen in their support of sites or local teams between meetings and then subsequently debrief after the meeting about what went on and how it might have been improved. They also set the agenda for the time between visits and for the next meeting. These people will be asked to stay in touch with the facilitator and any assistants throughout the project.

6. Publishing support for the final reports, which includes publication costs, copy editing, and binding, as well as distribution as desired by the sponsoring company. We have found that the

Reflective Questions

✦ What are your ideas on how to approach the parent organization regarding the support you will need?

✦ What challenges do you anticipate, and how do you plan to deal with them?

official publication of the work greatly enhances the quality of the solutions. Everyone likes to feel like his or her work has a legacy to help others in similar situations.

How Is the Hub and Spoke Participatory Action Research Design Employed for Dynamic Change or Reform?

How Do You Begin?

The first step for management is to work on finding some personal incentives that can be used to encourage people to take on the extra work that is being asked of them. This is a common problem for businesses, nonprofits, and public administrators, who generally expect that this kind of work should just be done under the normal auspices of a person's employment. We have found that incentives bring success, and without them, complex reforms of this nature are much more likely to experience a failure rate of somewhere around 50%. Here's why. This PAR process requires that these teams work outside of their normal business day to gather data, have meetings to discuss actions and measurements, implement new steps, and measure their success. You can consider them pilot projects in each of your major hubs of activity. If an organization hired consultants to work out a pilot for them, then those consultants would be paid. In this case, the staff should be treated with the same respect that would be given those consultants. The change in their attitudes will seem remarkable. When you are asking them to step up as experts in what they do and help you redesign their own working environment to better meet the needs of outside pressures to change and to pilot new ideas, and you show them respect by paying them extra for their extra work, they are much more likely to give it their full attention.

What are you asking them to do? They will be expected to participate regularly in an AR project and to write up the results in a final report that will be available to you for publication. This involves a discovery cycle where they analyze what needs to change in order to make your vision come true. Next, they present ideas as to which steps can be taken and measure the outcomes of those first steps. Finally, they come back and reflect with you on what they are finding. This then starts another round of discovery, measurable action, and reflection, a process that continues until you see real and sustainable change. In this manner, they take ownership of the changes needed and feel transformed in their new roles, and over time, you will be amazed at how much can be done and what positive attitudes will develop. The requirement for a final report is a necessary capstone to this kind of change process. We have found that the two elements that create success are the incentives and the requirement for a final report that will be published. The first shows respect; the second sets a high professional standard.

For a detailed facilitation guide, see Appendix D, which outlines a large-scale networked project where a national entity wants to create change in many areas.

Action Research for Business, Nonprofit, and
Public Administration

How Do People Connect in a Networked Design?

Networks self-organize; therefore, no outside party will ever be able to control the communication pattern or the way people connect in an NPAR project. Nevertheless, what matters is that you capture as much of the thoughts and communication between participants as possible. Fortunately, the three steps of discovery, measurable action, and reflection offer potential for setting up agreed-upon protocols to do most of the work for you. Simply discuss as a larger group how each of the small subgroups will keep the rest informed of what they are doing during each of the three steps.

We have found that the simplest and most successful way to ensure standard communication documentation is to have all participants agree to filling out the reflective protocol, discussed in an earlier chapter, once a week. As you well remember, the document is divided into three sections, one for each of the three AR steps. At the end of each week, every participant merely fills out what they have discovered, what measurable actions they may have taken, or any reflections they may have had on thoughts or feelings about the project and how it is progressing.

Friendships will form, subgroups will begin to work together, and people will naturally gravitate toward each other during a long-term PAR process. No one would want to constrain that natural progression. The weekly reflective protocol should capture the benefits of the liaisons for the record. The important thing is for the student or consultant facilitators to

Reflective Questions

- ✦ What are your ideas about the teams you might create? Who would be on the teams? How many teams might you have?
- ✦ What type of incentives would you ideally like to provide to team members? What would be reasonable and possible incentives?
- ✦ What resistance do you anticipate from team members? What are your ideas on how to deal with this?

have a means by which they communicate personally and individually back to either the small-group teams or the individuals. These communications need to be recorded as they become data and may later influence what measurable actions are implemented based on what outcomes are reported. It is important to remember that this is a new skill for the participants and that regular feedback is essential for them to connect with the process. Once they do, though, the results are outstanding as is shown in the following quote from one of our participants:

> With AR you do acquire the knowledge, and engage in it. Once I got into the involvement pieces things totally came together, I started out wanting to look at one thing and ended with a completely different understanding, you go back to the process for support—I had read about it, but now for me it was real because I was experiencing it. I saw it, I had real life examples, it was almost as if a marionette was up there orchestrating these wonderful experiences for me. (Brent, 2006)

Does a Network Have to Preexist or Can You Start One for the Project?

We have been involved in two major networked AR projects. Neither one of them had a network in place when we started. One was successful, and one was not, but both might have been more successful had we been able to roll out our ideas into an existing network. Why? Because longer association might provide more glue or connection to hold the group together. The single biggest challenge is whether you can keep people motivated throughout the project.

Reflective Questions

- ✦ How will you ensure that participants are tracking their data regularly and uniformly?
- ✦ How will you personally communicate back to the teams or individuals? How will this be recorded so you can use it as data?

Action Research for Business, Nonprofit, and Public Administration

The issue of building connections is essentially the critical point. That is the reason we suggest that large reform projects always have incentives that are large enough to keep people motivated to attend. That way, they feel connected to the outcome for personal reasons, which may balance a desire to stop during some of the rougher spots of the implementation process. Other types of incentives include large social or economic goals that everyone wants to see their community or network attain. Some successful examples follow.

Are There Examples of Networked Participatory Action Research?

We first implemented the hub and spoke design in a national project in the United States that was focused on improving education for students who were temporarily without homes or whose families moved frequently due to poverty. The hub during the first year of the project was a meeting that occurred on a Saturday every 2 months. Upon researching the study after it was finished, we found that coming back together regularly increased everyone's sense of accountability to the project and was a necessary part of the design. The spokes were individual schools, and each attending team included the principal and a teacher. In subsequent years, the team was expanded to also include a community member. Individual schools were encouraged to pursue outcomes in their own ways in their local contexts, thus contributing to our understanding of a wide variety of specific ways in which education could be improved for these marginalized children.

Reflective Questions

- ✦ Do you know of an already formed network that you plan to use, or are you going to create your own?
- ✦ What do you think will be the pros and cons of each situation?

This project continued and spread across the United States, employing an online format. These groups were somewhat less successful as they had to simultaneously deal with learning how to communicate online and complete their own projects. In subsequent years, the project was kicked off with one face-to-face meeting and then continued online. Results were strong but never as robust as that first year when people met face-to-face on a regular basis.

A student project that took the form of NPAR took place in Marion County, Oregon, as a networked team faced the challenges of human trafficking. This PAR team was part of a wider initiative and was made up of individuals who were interested in the topic from diverse organizations within the community and a few from neighboring states. The hub for this team was a regular meeting sponsored by the county, where other subcommittees were also in attendance. The committee employing PAR was by far the most successful, and when asked why, they replied, "Having a defined process allowed us to come back to our purpose and really focus on where we were and where we were going when we got off track" (Carter, 2010).

The spokes in this design were sometimes competing organizations that were able to lay down any animosity or miscommunication to work and achieve the greater good; in this case, increased legal protection for the victims of trafficking and increased consequences for the perpetrators. Their own words follow:

Action Research for Business, Nonprofit, and Public Administration

This team obtained valuable education and information in our quest to partner in a way that helped us to develop creative suggestions for transferring immediate accountability from victims to perpetrators of human trafficking in Marion County, Oregon. We identified limitations and barriers that can be remedied with initial start up funding for intensive training and education for a team of intervention providers. Once trained, these providers will be able to provide offender intervention services designed for immediate financial and behavioral accountability. Our team suggests polygraph examinations as an intervention too. Further that all perpetrators be held financially responsible for their services and that any revenue be shared with victim services to expand support and law enforcement services to extend funding for ongoing sting operations. (Carter, 2010)

Is NPAR successful? In the words of a school administrator from the first project,

As an administrator, if I felt frustrated that teachers weren't doing what I wanted them to do, then I might consider PAR because it gets them involved in "doing." Are there other reasons I would choose it for professional development? Because it will help the school to be more effective, you can tailor it to the situation. You can get the data to support the issues, or find an assumption. For us, I know we haven't done a good enough job of assessing data, but going and telling them that won't make that happen. I will need to guide my staff to find out for themselves where it is that we're missing the target, then they'll own the process, be excited about it and make some changes. (Drobney, 2005)

Reflective Questions

✦ What ideas or thoughts did these two examples bring to your mind?
✦ How might you learn from these examples when doing your own project?

How Could Virtual Tools, Learning Management Systems, or Social Networking Platforms Be Used to Your Network's Advantage?

Travel is expensive, and even people working in the same office may not have time to meet regularly. Therefore, it is important that the group discuss how often they need to see each other versus what communication can go on online. There are a number of tools that you might consider, as others have found them useful.

Virtual Tools

While the selection of virtual tools is constantly expanding, some that we have found helpful include: an online drop box where people can share documents simultaneously and easily, an online meeting room where one person can lead a live discussion with a video camera and others participate through audio or text, or Skype where one or more people can chat or discuss things face-to-face using web cameras and video. The importance of the employment of any virtual tool is dependent on two criteria: first, that it is easy enough to use so that it does not frustrate people more than they can easily tolerate, and second, that it fits the task for minimal (if any) cost.

Learning Management Systems

Because the hub is much like a classroom where people meet, discuss ideas, look over documents together, and so on, a learning management online tool can be employed as that central meeting place for the group. It has been our experience, however, that asynchronous discussion (where people go online at different times) should not be the only option but rather should be augmented with some live meetings as well.

Social Networking Platforms

Facebook or Google groups are probably the biggest social networking platforms, although there are others. To employ them, it is important that everyone knows how to use them and that everyone maintains the proper level of confidentiality if that is important to your group. The advantages can be an increased sense of connection as people can quickly understand what is going on in other people's projects, make comments, and employ those ideas in their own projects if they desire.

No matter how you structure your NPAR groups, you can expect some natural ebb and flow of communication and interest during the project. Naturally, the closer connections, the higher stakes, the shorter time, or the greater incentives will all heighten the possibility of more positive growth and less challenge. It is important to recognize that global networks are very difficult to bend to the will of any one set of desired outcomes. Attrition is always difficult in PAR. It becomes monstrous in global and diverse situations unless the group is tied together with bonds stronger than mutually desired outcomes. Coghlan and Coughlan (2006) describe a network where everyone was part of a common supply chain. Their project worked because

Reflective Questions

✦ What is your experience with virtual tools, learning management systems, and social networking platforms?
✦ How do you see these things fitting into your project?

grant money from the European Union (EU) provided their services and resources for the project. Some extrinsic motivation needs to be present, or holding a group to a single focused task becomes impossible when up against competing divergent responsibilities.

Conclusion

This chapter discussed some of the practical considerations involved in conducting PAR in network environments. The definition of a network for our purposes was stated as a group of people connected to one another, either in a face-to-face situation or aided by some type of technology. It's possible that the people in the network may not know each other before the project.

There is evidence for why using NPAR can be advantageous when trying to roll out reform or change efforts. Networks have certain attributes that have shown to be beneficial in these types of situations. These attributes include increased levels of creativity that occur in groups, as well as increased interconnectedness and transparency. The hub and spoke design has been discussed as optimal for PAR projects within a network.

The facilitator or student needs to either find existing networks or create their own. To employ the hub and spoke design, small teams must be created who all convene together at the designated hub. These teams both bring information into the hub from their various locations and also back out from the hub to their local environments. These teams are expected to put a lot of work into the PAR project, and so it is essential to the success of the project that they be compensated in some way. Incentives are useful to motivate team members and increase buy-in for the project. The facilitator needs to work on all these issues as well as issues of regular and uniform data collection. Communication in an NPAR project is key and must be captured as a form of data. This included the facilitator's communication back to the team members. There are many tools that may be helpful to the project, including virtual tools, learning management systems, and social networking.

Take Action

- Decide whether you will use an existing network or create your own.

- Come up with a draft of who will be on your small teams and where the hub will be.

- Come up with a list of possible incentives for the team members.

- Create a plan that outlines how communication will be used as data in your project. Make sure your plan ensures regular and uniform data collection.

- Decide how you will use virtual tools, learning management systems, and social networking in your project.

Additional Readings

Brown, L. D., & Gaventa, J. (2010). Constructing transnational action research networks: Reflections on the Citizenship Development Research Centre. *Action Research, 8*(1), 5–28.

Fuller-Rowell, T. E. (2009). Multi-site action research: Conceptualizing a variety of multi-organization practice. *Action Research, 7*(4), 363–384.

Haslett, T., Barton, J., Stephens, J., Schell, L., & Olsen, J. (2010). Leadership in a network learning: Business action research at Monash University. *The Learning Organization, 17*(1), 104–116.

Medaglia, R. (2007). Measuring the diffusion of eParticipation: A survey on Italian local government. *Information Polity: The International Journal of Government & Democracy in the Information Age, 12,* 265–280.

Chapter 7.
Analyzing and
Reporting Results

Results for AR happen on two levels: the personal transformational process that most researchers experience and their findings and conclusions, which as with any research, may have importance to others facing similar dilemmas. In order for the results to have importance, they need to be convincing to others. Not all research is successful in that regard, and that does not make it bad research; in fact, it is as valuable to report failure, with a detailed explanation of what caused your work to fail, as it is to report success. After all, the legacy of failed projects can be to improve other people's practice, and we do that as much by illuminating what caused our difficulties as we do through touting real (and sometimes imagined) successes. This chapter discusses the analysis of your project data so that your results are convincing and then how to take those results and report them to others, whether your project was fully successful, partially successful, or failed.

This chapter will discuss the two types of outcomes, personal and public, as tacit and explicit knowledge. Prior to looking objectively at your data, we will suggest you analyze your personal lessons. These can be celebrated over and above what may or may not have happened with your research as it is likely that, through your reflexions and reflections, you will notice that you have grown both personally and professionally in many ways. In our personal work with AR as professional development, we found that it is experienced by most practitioners as at least somewhat transformational and that feelings of learning accompany reflective cycles where you discuss your growth in emotional intelligence (reflexivity) as well as your deepest critical responses to your work (reflection) (Goleman, 2006a, 2006b).

It may be the comingling of your personal results with your research results that causes AR to be seen as *soft* research. A member of a collaborative AR network was overheard to say at a conference, "We have to question why all of the research in this matter was successful." Rather than have others question the credibility of your findings as research, you will want to separate the personal from the professional and report them accordingly.

In the service of helping you write the best possible final report for your stakeholder population, this chapter discusses analysis from two points of view—personal and professional—and then goes on to discuss how to report the latter to your stakeholders.

Chapter 7 will address the following questions:

- How do I assess my research outcomes?

- How do I analyze my work as data?

- Success or failure, how do I tell them apart?

- What standards do I need to hold for final analysis?

- How do I pull my analysis into the seven concepts discussed in research?

- How do I write the best report for my stakeholders?

- What if my stakeholders need to see success, but I am less than happy with my results?

How Do I Assess My Research Outcomes?

AR adds to both personal and professional knowledge and capacity to act. Knowledge is generally divided into two types: explicit and tacit. Explicit knowledge is that which can be articulated into formal language and measured or debated by others. It is organized through cognitive processes and reasoning and is most of what we talk about when we mention analyzing data. Tacit knowledge is personal, embedded in our individual experiences, and is much of what we talk about when we discuss reflexion. This section is concerned with both.

Analysis and reporting are alchemical processes through which the researcher takes into themselves all of their experiences and reflects on them deeply, and a completely new version of what happened emerges from the reflection. To what extent that new embodiment of the work is convincing or important to others has a great deal to do with how deeply you answer the question, "How do I know what I did?" Therefore, we suggest three different methods of sorting through the evidence you have collected. Each way of looking at data will draw up a different perspective, and the pulling apart of these perspectives leads to greater wisdom.

Step 1: Reflect Upon Your Personal Journey

Lay out your weeks of reflective data side by side. It is illuminating to read from left to right across the weeks all of the things that you discovered. Then, sit back, and reflect upon the new tacit knowledge that may have changed you as a person, your ideas, or your understanding of the context of your work. Wicks and colleagues (2008) discuss how most AR is done out of "a desire to contribute towards a better future" (p. 23). After a while, do the same thing with what you wrote under measurable actions. In retrospect, to what extent do you believe that your new tacit understanding and improved skills will help you personally? To what extent do you believe the project's measurable actions will contribute to the better world you envision? What were the challenges you faced? What would you do differently next time? How has all of this made you a better researcher? Finally, again after a period of time, read all of your reflections. Do you have evidence that you have grown as a person? What are your feelings as you end the project?

If you were going to celebrate one aspect of your tacit, personal success with this project, what would it be? Seldom is there a student in the class who does not leave the class chatting about all the things that they have learned. Revel in your personal development. Talk about what happened to you with others. It is only by clearly separating how good we feel about our personal lessons that we can come to neutral objectivity when we move on to analyze our work as research.

Step 2: Reflect on Your Beginning Purpose

At the beginning of your AR project, you likely wrote a proposal. In that proposal, you expressed the purpose of your work most often as the situation you wanted to improve or something you wanted to learn or put into action. Therefore, the first natural sorting mechanism is to go through all of your data and code, or separate, all of the parts that show movement toward or away from a positive outcome of your purpose.

Sometimes, that cyclic nature of AR takes us down unexpected pathways, and you may find that, while you did not have great success in addressing your original purpose, your purpose has shifted and the outcomes you sought were redefined. AR can be a messy process. It remains for you to report what happened to your stakeholders in such a way that they are convinced. If, for instance, your stakeholders are research professionals, you will need to disclose your process that led to the change. If your stakeholders are businesspeople with busy schedules, you may not want to take valuable time in your final report on the details of how you got to where you are—you can leave that for when and if they ask you about it.

Finish this process by completing a new reflective protocol. What have you discovered about your success or failure in achieving your purpose?

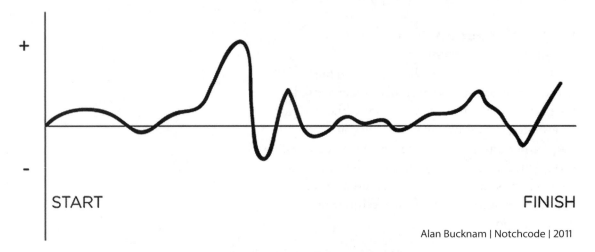

MOVING TOWARD A POSITIVE OUTCOME

+

−

START

FINISH

Alan Bucknam | Notchcode | 2011

MOVING AWAY FROM A POSITIVE OUTCOME

Figure 7.1 illustrates how tracking movement toward or away from a positive outcome can help to refine your approach.

How would you quantify those results in terms of explicit knowledge? How could you tell others about it, and where are the measurements that make it convincing? What measurable outcomes are you proud of?

And, what do you wish you had been able to accomplish that remains outside of your grasp? What were the challenges you faced? And, what would you tell others facing the same challenges?

Action Research for Business, Nonprofit, and Public Administration

Step 3: Chart Your Measurable Actions

Now that the work is over, you can plot it on a timeline or chart. The lower left-hand corner is where you started or your baseline, which you measured at the beginning in some detail. In regular increments, your project moved across time. In many cases, it also evolved upward from the baseline. By reading your weekly reflective protocols and the measurable actions section of those, you can complete a chart or graph that graphically shows the evolution of your work. If you put your purpose or the outcome you hoped to achieve in the upper right-hand corner, you will have a graphic display of how you see the outcomes of your work in comparison to what you had hoped for at the beginning.

Taken together, these three processes should help you do two things. First, you should be able to separate your personal (tacit knowledge) from your professional (explicit) outcomes and move to a greater level of neutrality in your reporting of them. Second, you should understand from a neutral stance whether you will be reporting small success, great success, or failure. You now know what your report will say, and you can move on to weaving the evidence you have into a convincing story that correctly displays your outcomes to your stakeholders.

Note that you may choose to report your increases in tacit and explicit knowledge together as in Margolin (2007), who first described her personal internal transformation, which lead to her taking on new styles of collaborative work within her organization.

Reflective Questions

✦ When you do a beginning analysis of your results, what can you say are your tacit or explicit outcomes?

✦ Does your analysis show a relationship between the growth of explicit and tacit understanding?

✦ What did you do at the beginning of your project that either made these analyses easier or more difficult?

✦ What might you do differently next time?

REFLECT ON YOUR PERSONAL JOURNEY:

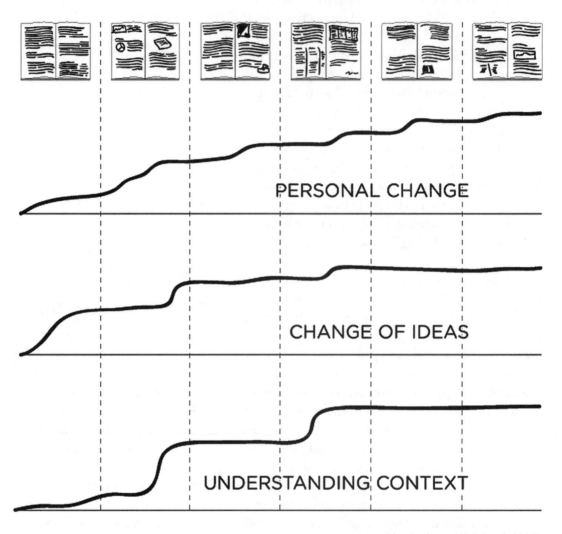

Alan Bucknam | Notchcode | 2011

Figure 7.2 illustrates how using journal entries helps to analyze and report on results in your own personal journey during the project.

Action Research for Business, Nonprofit, and
Public Administration

These shifts resulted in new explicit actions that led to further conclusions and tacit understanding of the value of distributed leadership. If and to the extent that your analysis reveals such a back-and-forth between the tacit and the explicit, between the reflexive and the strategic, then your report needs to reflect that relationship.

How Do I Analyze My Work as Data?

Like alchemy, analysis is a cumulative process—one that cannot be completed without the "right" ingredients. At the end of the project, practitioners must show that the opinions they have formed about the legitimacy of their results are logical and accurate, following naturally from data collected during the process. For this reason, as has been the case with other researchers (Creswell, 2009; Maxwell, 1996; Patton and Patton, 2002; Strauss and Corbin, 1998; Thomas, 2003), we suggested at the start that you contemplate the types of information you would need for your particular set of stakeholders. The use of your reflective notes, in conjunction with the evidence you collected during your measurable action steps, make the end stage of this process less daunting. Your findings develop from cumulative records of all data collected over the course of your project, and because you designed that with your stakeholders in mind, you should have all you need.

Deeper analysis as a researcher is now required. Once again, lay out all of your reflective data week by week, side by side, but this time, also cluster around it other data or evidence that will substantiate or add to your final report. These might include surveys, interview data, and so on. What you have in front of you is a graphic representation of all the bits and pieces that you can use to build your final report.

Some researchers find that, when they lay out all the evidence they have, there are things that they know but don't yet have evidence for. Therefore, a quick flurry of activity back to their contexts for further research may be well advised. Before final report writing, you need to have substantiated evidence for every lesson that has come from your work. These lessons are otherwise called findings and answer the questions you had when you started. Findings always need to be backed up with data.

At this point, you have the opportunity to use both another objective set of eyes and those of someone in your group to double-check your findings. Called interrater reliability (when an outside party codes and checks the coding of your data) and member checks (when a group member substantiates your findings), these two steps greatly increase the credibility and validity of your results.

Conclusions develop from your findings. At the end of any research, the researcher sits back and asks, "What does it all mean? What is the significance of it? What would my message be to others?" Analysis, if well done, draws you naturally through your data to your findings and then, with a little reflection, on to your conclusions. You may consider allowing some of your tacit knowledge to be included in your conclusions; if so, then you need to be clear that these developed from reflexive moments.

The following exercise was published in our first book, and students reported that it was instrumental in their success when reporting data as findings and moving on to conclusions:

1. Sort your data into categories of lessons learned or outcomes you can claim.

2. List under each category the data that confirm that lesson. Also, list any data that refute this claim.

3. Compare this list to the questions you asked or to your purpose, then rank order the categories with the ones closest to 1 being the most credible to others as meeting the claim that you accomplished your purpose. The top should be the one lesson that has the most confirmation and the least refuting data. These become your findings.

4. If you worked in a group, discuss your findings with your colleagues, and question whether your rank order and findings match what they would consider to be important.

5. Decide whether you (and your team members) met or exceeded the purpose of your study. How do the specific findings add up (or not) to your achievement of the purpose of your research?

Reflective Questions

+ To what extent do your data lay out in a logical trail back to your purpose?

+ If your project took a few twists and turns, how will you report them?

+ What resources (people, books, websites) do you think might be able to help you with this deeper analysis of your data?

6. Reflect and ask yourself the following: What does it all mean? What is the significance of it, explicitly and tacitly? What would my message be to others?

7. Draft a few statements of conclusion from the answers to those questions. Discuss your conclusions with the rest of your group if you worked with one.

8. Outline the most logical way to discuss the progression from your categorical findings to your conclusions.

Success or Failure, How Do I Tell Them Apart?

By now, you should have a pretty good idea about whether you feel you can substantiate that your project was successful from a research standpoint. Please note that this is separate from the fact that it may have been successful in terms of your increased knowledge of conducting AR and that it may have led to a personally transformational experience. Success, as we are talking about it here, is measured solely in terms of the data as it relates to your initial purpose. Do you know a lot more about your topic than you did when you started? Does this leave you (or the people you are working with) better able to solve the problem(s) on which your research was focused? Three possible categories emerge for reporting: great success, medium or small success, and no success or failure.

Before going into this analysis, we should note that often the difference between these distinctions is whether the researcher has more time to continue the cycles of AR. Presumably, almost any project could enjoy positive outcomes given enough time for fine tuning and reorganization.

Great Success

If you met or exceeded your purpose and can demonstrate it with data, then you can and should claim great success. An example of a student's work that can make this claim includes the nurse who completed a preliminary design for a database to be used by families with members who had special needs. This

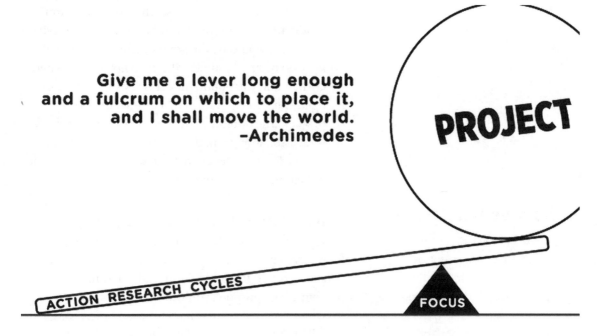

Alan Bucknam | Notchcode | 2011

Figure 7.3 demonstrates that, if you have time to complete additional cycles of research, you can leverage even the most unwieldy projects into successful outcomes.

database will allow emergency health care workers to know the specifics required in treatment by these family members, thus reducing potential disaster for people with special needs, especially in emergency situations. This student exceeded her purpose because, in the process of questioning people about the database, she found great enthusiasm and support throughout her community. She ended the project with others being willing to help make it happen.

Moderate or Small Success

If you came close to or can demonstrate clear outcomes that lead to a natural progression of your project toward your purpose, then you can claim moderate or small success. An example of this type of project would be the woman who called together a group of small municipalities to investigate whether they, and the public they serve, would benefit from their collaboration in a biofuel distillery project. The outcomes showed promising results for such a collaboration, but at the time of the report, there was no evidence that the municipalities would, in fact, move forward on the idea.

Interesting Project but Failed

If you found that there were more challenges in this research project than you had anticipated, or if data show that your work did not lead you directly to your target purpose, you will need to report that, while your project may have been very interesting, it failed. As mentioned before, failure in research is not a disaster but rather a lesson to be learned. Therefore, your purpose in reporting is to help others understand

Reflective Questions

- ✦ What are the moderate results that you might be able to change to positive outcomes given more time?
- ✦ Did you experience any failure in your research project? If so, how might you turn those lessons to success?

how you got off track or why you could not overcome the challenges you faced. An example of an interesting project but one that failed to meet its original purpose would be a student in homeland securities who was investigating activist groups in order to better understand the reasoning and logic that might pervade the establishment of a terrorist cell. While his work with political groups was interesting and he came to solid conclusions about how and why they form, the transference of that to terrorism remained elusive.

What Standards Do I Need to Hold for Final Analysis?

Research practice is typically measured against the standards of validity, credibility, and reliability. Together, measuring your results against these standards can help you make the argument that your findings and your conclusions are correct, and then your final report becomes more convincing to your audience. Valid, credible, and reliable are concepts applied with and beyond the research community, although they have very specific meanings within the quantitative research paradigm. As discussed, the final research and analysis are built upon the root of your reflective protocol throughout all the cycles of your AR process.

The world of research evaluation offers slightly different but complementary ideas. Researchers would say that analysis of the early research cycles provide *formative* results that affect later cycles. In other words, you build and grow as you go until the end. Herr and Anderson (2005) call this "designing the plane while flying it" (p. 69), and Wicks and colleagues (2008) mirror that sentiment when they discuss "make the road while walking" (p. 24). These ideas sync with the concepts of trustworthiness and authenticity as proposed by Guba and Lincoln (1985, 1986, 1989), who suggest that the positivistic standards of credible, valid, and reliable no longer fit, indeed, never fit the world of evaluation (and we would suggest are a hard fit for AR as well).

Now that you are ready to do your *summative* evaluation (done at the end of your study), you need to question whether you can make a claim for your work against any of the three original standards or the comparatively modern ideas of trustworthiness and authenticity. All of these concepts are discussed in the following sections.

Validity

AR has two overarching goals: (1) to increase personal and community knowledge about a topic of the study and (2) to show results of improvements or movement toward defined purpose (Anderson, Herr & Nihlen, 2005). To what extent the practitioner can demonstrate these two goals determines the **validity** of their claims. Your study may be valid in one area but not in the other, as discussed previously in this chapter when we separated your personal results from your professional. Anderson and colleagues go on to discuss several kinds of validity, each of which is a claim you could make in your final report. *Outcome* validity is whether you were successful in getting to your purpose.

Process validity discusses whether you can show that your research was well done, that it included the voices of others in the context, and that it met the standards of research as discussed throughout this book. *Democratic* validity is appropriate for PAR studies, and it demonstrates that the voices of all members of the community were considered. *Catalytic* validity is exemplified in the nurse's study in the previous section of this chapter. It is when one of your outcomes exceeds your target in one or more ways. Finally, *dialogic* validity can be claimed by the extent to which you can demonstrate that a diverse group of stakeholders were involved and now agree with your final conclusions and analysis. Dialogic validity requires a discussion of the ways in which others collaborated with you throughout the project and through analysis and report writing.

Credibility

There are two attributes that you need to consider as you write your final report in order to ensure its **credibility** to your stakeholders: how you report the data and how you report the process.

Data transformation is suggested by Creswell (2009) as a method through which mixed methodological research makes its credibility apparent to its constituency. Credibility (or whether your case is convincing) is the degree to which the person reading the report thinks that it makes sense. This is a subjective judgment and requires AR researchers to be cognizant of their audience and context. When applying concurrent qualitative and quantitative strategies, as is typical in most AR studies, both types of processes enhance the strength of the other. As has been discussed earlier, qualitative data such as interviews can be quantified by counting the number of times certain topics are discussed. Also, the percentages of individuals who agree to one thing or another quantifies qualitative evidence and makes it feel more solid, or credible, to the reader. Likewise, quantitative evidence can be qualified by discussing key phrases that were written as comments or adding quotations from interviews that agree with the finding that developed.

Both types of data measure specific ideas or variables that you will use to develop theories about the relationships you discovered through discussion of correlations that exist between them. For instance, to use the nurse's example in the previous section, as her work developed, it became clear that there were two issues with the database for special needs clients: the issue of the types of data that were needed would have to involve psychoemotional characteristics, and the issue of confidentiality. These became the nurse's variables. To make a report credible, she needed to pull together qualitative and quantitative data that discussed the community's thoughts about each. Reporting these data require reducing them, charting them, finding patterns between them, and then writing a comparison and contrast of all the elements you find.

A final report will not be credible unless documentation can be found and discussed both quantitatively and qualitatively. Why? When do you know that your data can stand on their own? This has to do with the humanity of your stakeholders. Some people are convinced by qualitative data and some people by quantitative numbers. In order to enhance the credibility of your final report, you will need both.

The second question that you have to consider is how or whether you are going to report your process. While action researchers enjoy the cycles of discovery, measurable action, and reflection, they are not inherently necessary in the final report. At the same time, there can be definite reasons that you need to explain the process in order to make what you found seem natural and, therefore, more credible to your audience. Surprising findings may hold the most value to your AR and to your constituency (Brause, 2000). Providing that your findings are valid, writing them up as part of the process that revealed them will add further credibility.

Reliability

There are two types of **reliability**: internal and external. There is the reliability that relates to following all good research practices and demonstrating one-to-one correlation between your data and your findings (internal reliability). Another test of reliability is whether these studies could be implemented in new settings (external reliability). We suggest that students follow the Lewis and Ritchie (2003) reliability test and explicitly discuss their analyses of the internal and external reliability of their findings. These may be discussed as part of findings or as part of limitations depending upon the outcome of these three questions:

1. Do the findings from the population queried accurately represent the entire population for which they are a part?

2. Can it be inferred that the findings from this study can be transferred to other locations or environments? To what extent do these findings provoke greater ideas about the larger field of study of which they are part? (Lewis & Ritchie, 2003, pp. 270–273)

When the things we study or the actions we take emerge from complex situations, AR results may not dependably transfer across settings (external reliability). This may not matter to you or your constituency as, in general, action researchers do not believe in one-size-fits-all types of solutions. That said, we also know the importance of businesspeople learning from each other. This can mean completely believing in the reliability of AR project results, if not to create a model for success, at least to provoke new and innovative ideas in business, nonprofit, and public administration. For this reason, we recommend reading the studies of other AR researchers. We believe that, as a result, you will discover valuable insights across a range of topics, including but not limited to leadership, organizational politics, organizational development issues, and economic and personnel factors in businesses, nonprofits and public administration offices. We also hope that you write up your final report in such a way as it adds to the body of literature that may help others.

Trustworthiness

Based upon the postmodern idea that there is no single reality but rather multiple realities that require an interweaving of individual "truths" to see the full picture, Guba and Lincoln (1985, 1986, 1989) developed the four principles of **trustworthiness** as an alternative set of standards against which evaluations (and we would say AR) could be judged. These four principles answer the following questions:

1. Does it demonstrate true value to the context from which it is taken?

2. Is it applicable to arenas outside of itself?

3. Are findings and conclusions consistent with the evidence?

4. Do findings and conclusions demonstrate neutrality?

Each of the four principles transfers into subtopics to include more conventional discussions of whether and to what extent your research demonstrates: prolonged engagement, persistent observation, cross-checking of data, peer debriefing, negative case analysis, and member checks.

Authenticity

The authors were not entirely satisfied with their first attempt to step out of the positivistic paradigm. As their work continued, they developed a parallel set of criteria through which we might judge the outcome of our AR project—that of its **authenticity.** We will lightly discuss their ideas of fairness, ontological authenticity, educative authenticity, and

Reading the studies of other AR researchers will help you to discover valuable insights across a range of topics, including leadership, organizational politics, organizational development issues, and economic and personnel factors across all sectors.

catalytic authenticity and then recommend that, if you are interested and think that analysis through the format of these ideas will be helpful to your case, follow through by reading Guba and Lincoln (1986) as listed in the additional readings and as available through EBSCO.

1. Fairness—did you, as the researcher, consider all sides and investigate all the possible interpretations of your situation? Does your final analysis do justice to each? Do you represent the values that underpin every opinion or positions on your topic?

2. Ontological authenticity—does your research aid yourself and others by growing overall consciousness in how all the parties see the world? Would you be able to say that everyone would feel they learned something? How would you justify this as truth?

3. Educative authenticity—does your research aid in the ability of people with disparate ideas to understand (if not agree with) opposing points of view?

4. Catalytic authenticity—did your work stimulate action toward the good of all?

Trustworthiness and authenticity are not mutually exclusive, and like the standards of credibility, validity, and reliability, both principles are interconnected, but your work may align with some standards and not fit well with others. These principles are merely a framework well developed by academic research through which you can show your AR project in its best light.

How Do I Pull My Analysis Into the Seven Concepts Discussed in Research?

Going back to our first discussion of the proposal in Chapter 2, you will remember that there are seven concepts always discussed in any type of research. They are purpose, scope, methodology, findings, conclusions, limitations, and contributions. If you wrote a proposal based upon those seven concepts, you can now revisit them and roll in your analysis to flesh out the beginning of your final report. Some things will not have changed, for example, your purpose. Likewise, but with small additions, you can now define your scope more accurately because that is the exact population that was included or influenced by your research.

Your methodology is still AR, but you will add to it the details of how many people were interviewed, who was included in the survey data, or any other specifics that came up along the way. You may or may not decide to illuminate how many cycles you did and what occurred in each cycle. That decision goes back to the previous section, when we discussed whether any of your findings were surprising. Basically, you will tell your readers or stakeholders about the specifics of your process only to the extent that it makes your findings and conclusions more convincing.

Reflective Questions

✦ What can you do to increase the likelihood of obtaining valid, credible, and reliable results?

✦ Will you also rate your work against the standards of trustworthiness and authenticity?

✦ What are some factors you might consider when deciding whether to include the AR process in your final report?

As was mentioned previously in this chapter, your findings must be shown to evolve naturally from your data, and these data can (and probably should) include your weekly reflective protocol. Your conclusions then are your personal evaluation of your findings as they have influence on your field of study. Limitations evolve out of your analysis of your validity, credibility, and reliability. Contributions can come out of your conclusions as to whether or to what extent your research impacts others.

Note here that you can have a very significant or even transformational contribution to your personal life, and it is valid to mention that in your contribution section. In fact, you can have two completely different sets of outcomes weaving their ways throughout all seven concepts as you discuss them in your final report. This is especially appropriate for a class situation as your stakeholder is your teacher. As was mentioned, there are two legitimate outcomes always on the table with AR: (1) to increase personal and community knowledge about a topic of this study and (2) to show results or improvements or movement toward defined purpose (Herr & Anderson, 2005).

How Do I Write the Best Report for My Stakeholders?

Anderson and colleagues (2005) discuss the politics of knowledge, institutional change, and professionalism. Each of these three puts pressures on your final report writing. As an example, you need to be aware of how you phrase results that may not be perceived as in alignment with current strategic directions. Also, you will consider potential pitfalls pointed out during your investigation or the tension between your role as researcher (and therefore expert in this situation) and your role as perceived within the organization (which refers back to our earlier discussions in Chapter 5 on insider research and on power).

It may be helpful to look at your report writing through the lens of the three AR steps.

Reflection

This process starts with the reflective practice that you implement just prior to writing your final report.

You have finished a series of AR cycles, and you have taken some small measurable action steps toward your purpose in doing the project. Now is the time to ask yourself the following:

1. What has been the biggest lesson?

2. What is the most compelling action or fact that you want others to hear about?

3. Is there a single message that you want to convey or a series of steps?

4. What is your single-sentence, bottom-line outcome or lesson?

5. Will your stakeholders find this interesting as well?

6. May your researchers find this threatening in some fashion?

It is also wise to spend some time reflecting on your stakeholders and their needs as it is likely that you have multiple people for whom your story will hold interest. Start by listing them, what ties they have in your work, what types of data they will likely find the most convincing, and the format you believe they would be most likely to use. Keep in mind the amount of time they have, the depth (or lack of depth) of the relationship they have with you and your work, and the best way you think you could attract them to the message you want to deliver.

As an example, if you have few ties to your stakeholders and they are busy people, then you likely have 30 seconds to deliver a message that is so compelling as to make them curious enough to grant you more time to satisfy their curiosity. On the other hand, if you have deep relationships, then they may grant you a length of time where you can meet face-to-face and discuss not only your findings and conclusions but the entire process. The visual story you would need to tell would be very different in these two scenarios.

Discovery

This leads you to a discovery cycle where your goal is to ascertain if your stakeholders already have a reporting structure in place that you need to follow. How does this compare with the natural suggestions that came to mind when you answered the questions about their connection with you, whether they were expecting or invested in your work, and the time they would likely give it? Strategically, if the two things don't jive, then you may want to try a dual angle of approach to final reporting.

Action Research for Business, Nonprofit, and
Public Administration

As an example, let's suggest that one of your stakeholders has power over a budget that would continue your work and that such a continuation would be advantageous from your point of view. Let's say that they have a formal reporting structure but that, because they have little active relationship with you, you are skeptical if they will give such a report much time or attention. This is a frequent dilemma and one that may require a two-pronged approach where you first find an advocate who gets you and your report in the door and then you back that up with a full, formal report.

Measurable Action

Now it is time to develop your first draft of your final report. Choose one of the four following possibilities, depending on your analysis of your stakeholders as mentioned previously.

1. The formal report is characterized by it being a written document and including the seven concepts that are in all types of research: purpose, scope, methodology, findings, conclusions, limitations, and contributions. This is appropriate for academics, funders, and publication in academic journals.

2. The formal presentation has the same ingredients as the formal report but also tells the story of what you have done (the AR), places it in the local context, and elaborates on the people involved. Woven together as more of a storytelling format, this reporting structure is appropriate for school boards, legislators, local businesspeople, committees or parent groups, and administrators.

3. The informal individual report is streamlined to your audience's needs. Perhaps this is one punchy message with a one-page overview for the busy stakeholder. This format is appropriate for speaking engagements and makes use of charts and brief language. Used in faculty meetings, conferences, and newsletters, this format presents facts in a clear and easily accessible manner.

4. The informal group report is most often a wall display or presentation that runs in the background of an event. It has limited contents as it focuses on the successes of the project and may be characterized by a press release format. This is most useful for the press, awards celebrations, dignitary speeches, and newsletters with stakeholder audiences in your local community.

Your measurement will be to test your report out on people who know your stakeholders and to get their responses. Remember, this is for feedback, so don't get defensive when they make corrective comments. Peer review always makes the final product stronger.

Your final measurable action will be to deliver your final report and then wait for your stakeholders' responses.

Final Reflections

There is an old saying that the work is not over until the paperwork is done. You may think that, with the completion of your reports to stakeholders, you can call it quits, but we suggest one final step. We have found that, after a final project is done, it is possible to access a deeper level of reflection. What have you really learned? More important, what would you have done differently, and what went so well that you would recommend it to others? These final personal truths are not available until you are looking back on the total package and able to reach some objectivity as you are no longer entangled in the project itself.

Almost like a final treat—a gift to yourself that will make your next project stronger—be sure to do one last overview. What did you discover (about yourself and the project)? What measurable actions made the most impact and why? Were there failures? What caused them? What were the limitations you faced? What are the implications or contributions of your work? Would you do it again? If so, what changes would you make?

With this you can put the report away, knowing that you have fished as much learning and knowledge out of it and the experience as you can. Now you are ready to go on to the next project!

What If My Stakeholders Need to See Success, but I Am Less Than Happy With My Results?

Finally, we should discuss the tension created in writing the final report when you do not believe that your stakeholders will be pleased by the results. Ethically, of course, you know that all data must

Reflective Questions

✦ Who are your stakeholders, and how will this affect the information you include in your final report?

✦ Considering your stakeholders, what are some possible challenges you may face in reporting, and what strategies could you use to overcome these?

be accurately reported. Nevertheless, there are gray areas within that. This book is written for business, nonprofits, and public administration, all of which make it common that there may be a possibility that a report will be received in a negative manner if its conclusions are not within the realm of being politically correct. These are murky waters, and while ethically, as researchers, we always report what we know, in a utilitarian sense, we do not want to be the messenger who gets shot because of the message.

Chris Argyris (1990) did a lot of work on defensive behaviors and points out in his analysis of the accident with the space shuttle *USS Challenger* in 1986, where the entire crew were killed. His report discovered that engineers had known there were challenges with the design but were unable to voice them due to a work environment where messengers of bad tidings were eliminated. True leadership involves ways in which to involve people in situations so that they can see for themselves what is being dealt with. Should any of our readers find themselves in an uncomfortable situation, we would hope that, rather than write a report that leaves out the negative, you would choose instead to invite into your AR world the stakeholder who will need convincing.

Three steps may prove helpful:

1. Approach the stakeholder in question privately with your results to obtain advance approval to report them.

2. Critically analyze your findings, and report on conflicting views about the results.

3. Have people who would naturally disagree
    with your findings review your drafts.

In each of these steps, you open yourself up to
learning from what may be an opposing point of
view. Your goal is to be able to present an accurate
report, which may involve some unpopular findings while causing as little political upheaval as
possible. It is likely that your findings have the
possibility of leading to some needed adjustments,
but when feathers are ruffled or feelings are hurt,
this may be more difficult to accomplish. In the
interest of getting your voice and the voice of your
work out, it can be beneficial to spend some time
trying to work with those who might object or be
offended by your findings. It may help to focus on
what you really think needs to be said in the report,
what will have the greatest positive impact, and
how to get that message across in the least offensive
way possible. To the extent you can incorporate
alternative positions without watering down your
conclusions, your work has the potential to make a
greater difference.

Nevertheless, most of our readers are students, and
your task is to convince your primary stakeholder,
your professor, of the credibility of your work. First,
you have to know what he or she is looking for. If
they need you to demonstrate increased professional
development, then slant your report that way. The
same would hold true for a professor looking for
emancipatory results in your organization, increased
levels of democracy, personal and professional critical reflexion and reflective reasoning, or any of the
other typical AR outcomes.

If you do not have gold-quality standard results, then it will do you well to report the pros and cons of your research, warts and all. The necessary point is that you learned from what may have been incorrect strategy. If your AR would have been contained in the "real" world of your work, you would have simply conducted a few more cycles in order to correct your early mistakes. Therefore, a natural conclusion would be that, with an extension of time, you would be able to do just that. We are sure that your professor will be excited by both what you have personally and professionally learned through this research; therefore, be sure that your findings and conclusions are credible across both of the previously discussed general purposes of the work: (1) to increase personal and community knowledge about a topic of this study and (2) to show results or improvements or movement toward defined purpose (Herr & Anderson, 2005).

Conclusion

During your project, you have come to appreciate how AR allows for continuous analysis by following three steps. The ability to benefit our organizations and world by making continuous progress is what distinguishes AR from other types of research. At the end of your AR project, you will inevitably need to do a final analysis of your work and create a report or several reports. This chapter covered some of the concrete steps that you will need to take in this process as well as some of the things you need to take into consideration as you make decisions about how to report your results.

AR is sometimes viewed as "soft" research, which may be due to the personal aspects involved in this type of work. We recommend a process in which you can fully explore the personal transformation, learning, and other results that occurred during your AR project while separating out the academic or professional results. When you have explored and separated your tacit knowledge, then you will have an easier time exploring, analyzing, and reporting on the explicit knowledge gained in your project.

Inherent in the AR process is a continuous type of analysis, which you will have carefully documented as you went along. At the end of the project, you will need to compile and look at the process as a whole. We have provided several methods and tools for you to use in laying out your data in order to view it in different ways. After using these tools to analyze your data, you will need to decide the level of success that your project had. Remember that this success refers strictly to the extent to which you met your original purpose and does not include any personal successes you may have experienced in the process. Also, remember that failure to attain your original purpose does not actually mean failure but is an opportunity to learn from mistakes.

In your final analysis, you will need to carefully consider the validity, credibility, and reliability of your project. These criteria are very important to academic work and will also help build your case for other stakeholders that you may have to report to at the end of this process. In addition, you may want to revisit the seven concepts of research that you used when writing your proposal. These concepts can help guide the format of your report if you are writing a formal report. If you will not be writing a formal report, then you can use the guidelines presented in this chapter to determine which type of reporting format best suits your needs.

When creating your final report, there are many things to consider, including what your stakeholders are looking for. It may be that they have a predetermined format for reporting that you will have to use. When creating a report for a professor, you should make sure you understand his or her guidelines and also what he or she is hoping you will focus on in your report. Your report should be geared toward the focus of the class and your professor's expectations. You may want to review with him or her the expectations mentioned by other professors at the beginning of Chapter 8; these can be stepping-off places for what you will need to include in your final document.

You will also need to be aware of any political implications of the report and be open to the possibility that your report will not be well received by some people. Remember that you are accountable to ethical standards requiring that you accurately report the findings of your study even if they may be unpopular. However, there are things that you can do in the reporting process that can help guide the reception of your report. You can take care to involve any potential adversaries in your reporting process to try and avoid future problems. Keep in mind that your report will do the most good if you can find a way to get your message across without creating enemies who may work to hide or discredit your work.

Finally, when you have created and distributed your final report, make sure to take some time to do some final reflections on the project as a whole. This final analysis will help draw the project to a close and will be helpful to you in your future AR endeavors.

Take Action

This chapter includes guidelines on how to proceed with your analysis and reporting. If you are finished with your project, then you can use this chapter to accomplish the following:

- Separate your tacit from explicit knowledge by exploring the personal aspects of your project.

- Analyze all of the data from your project in an academic manner, and decide on your level of success.

- Make sure to address validity, credibility, and reliability in your analysis and report.

- Decide what type of report you will need to create based on your stakeholders.

- Create and distribute your report(s).

- Do a final reflection after you have completed your final report.

Additional Readings

Argyris, C. (2002). Teaching smart people how to learn. *Reflections (1524–1734), 4(2),* 4.

Guba, E. G., & Lincoln, Y. S. (1986). *But is it rigorous? Trustworthiness and authenticity in naturalistic evaluation* (Vol. 30). San Francisco: Jossey Bass.

James, P., & Gittins, J. W. (2007). Local landscape character assessment: An evaluation of community-led schemes in Cheshire. *Landscape Research, 32,* 423–442.

Chapter 8.
Final Touches and
Emancipatory Potential

Now we come to the end of our journey through the practical considerations faced when doing AR. Key issues that will make or break your success include not only how you do AR but how you tie those actions together with the methodology through reflexion, reflection, and a coherent discussion of theory.

We return here to the theme of the emancipatory potential of AR to free and transform the researcher, the local situation, and sometimes even to reshape the workings of the world as experienced around the project. While your first AR projects will likely be more narrowly focused, aimed at completing a project at your university using this methodology, we want to close by reminding you of the vast potential that can develop from those narrow beginnings. We leave this volume hoping that, to the extent you are interested in making a broader mark on your world, you follow through by taking advantage of the various additional readings suggested at the end of each chapter. These will illustrate ways in which AR is used to influence a broader range of potential change than you will have been able to address in a short period of time.

Whether and to what extent you, our reader, employ this methodology to improve the quality or conditions around you, or the degree to which you use it to clean up complex situations, will depend upon your experiences employing AR as methodology. It is our sincere hope that this book will help you through whatever rough spots you face so that your experience is a good one and that you will help AR spread throughout the worlds of business, nonprofit, and public administration.

This chapter contains three sets of last words—from the three roles that intersect in this book. The words of AR teachers from around the world start this chapter by outlining cautions as to what defines greatness in AR rather than mere practice. They discuss what they hope you have learned and what their experience has taught them may be the hurdles you will face. Second, we ask our students a range of questions to uncover what they have learned from the process that might be helpful to you. And finally, we, the authors, take a small amount of space outlining what we hope may be next steps, not only for your work but for action researchers around the world and through the research world in order for all our work to offer the highest possible traction in the complex world we all face.

What Do the Teachers Say?

Instructors and professors who answered our query into what they hope their students get out of their first AR projects said the following:

1. For undergraduates or graduates starting a new career, AR gives you a chance to focus on something that matters—something special just to you—that you can talk about with confidence. Students in business, nonprofits, and public administration all come better prepared to discuss

specific aspects of their work environments due to having completed an AR project.

2. This can be an important contribution to your search for employment as the individual aspects of the project set you apart from others with the same degree and background.

3. For in-service practitioners and graduate students, AR not only engages you in something of personal importance but helps you gain an understanding of the theoretical underpinning of research, hopefully to influence your way of working to critically engage with the issues you face.

4. Should you be using AR as the primary methodology of your doctoral work, you can start your data collection earlier, complete several iterations, and finish with a career-enhancing project focused on having made a difference in your industry.

Emancipatory or Transformative Potential

We would like to expand on those last points by paraphrasing one of the greatest teachers of AR, who describes the essence of AR as a vehicle for transformation. Stephen Kemmis (2006) would add that students (and all of us) can improve our work through the following:

1. Reaching beyond the focus on improving techniques of practice to address the broader questions about how work influences the

Addressing broader questions about how work influences the context in society allows our research to become a vehicle for world-improving debate.

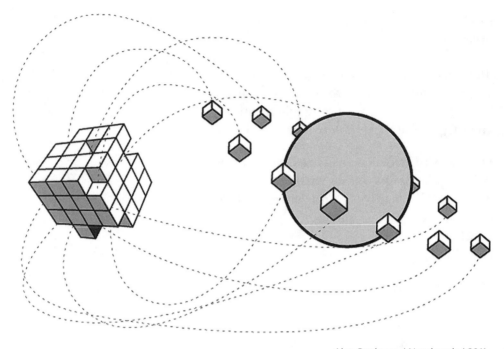

Alan Bucknam | Notchcode | 2011

Figure 8.1 illustrates the expansive potential of AR as per Kemmis (2006).

context in society, becoming a vehicle for critical debate to improve our world.

2. Reaching beyond a focus on improving efficiency to one of taking a critical view on the "irrational, unjust or alienating consequences of contextual issues that cause the issues our projects address" (p. 460).

3. Using AR to improve policy beyond something that creates conformity to build flexible structures that can be used to address everyone's needs.

4. Reaching beyond improved understanding of the situation only from the professional's point of view to one that is inclusive of the needs and ideas of community members and the broader public.

5. Reaching beyond acting alone to becoming part of the wider AR community so that your work adds to the discursive commentary on what we do and how to make it work better, expanding the knowledge about AR in the world (a point to which we will come back at the end of this chapter).

How Are These Improvements Made?

First, incorporate theoretical ideas throughout your work. Although this text consciously focuses on the how-to-do questions of AR, we agree with other professors who have stated that students' work can improve through reflection as well as linking practice to theory. To do this, we suggest all students use this book as it was designed, as an adjunct to other works (many of which are referenced here) that focus on the theoretical issues faced by practitioners of AR.

"Where their work could almost always improve is in having a more critical understanding, more evidently using critical thinking and thereby unpacking deeper layers of meanings for their findings and claims. For many student action researchers, it would be an improvement if they understood AR as epistemology or philosophy and not methodology. So, they could benefit intellectually from doing more philosophy. After 20 years as an action researcher, I still consider myself to be a student of its possibilities for praxis, improving social justice and helping me to identify and live by my values" (Parker, personal communication, 2011).

Second, continue to work on your own reflexivity and reflections. In various sections throughout this book, we have developed the idea of when your practice needs to be reflexive as well as reflective, and we have encouraged you to capture both in journals so as to use them as data.

"Writing reflexions (how you respond to the situations you face as part of your research) and reflections (your feelings and ideas about your research and all that it contains) is something I discovered takes time and depends on many aspects of the student's background. Science students, for example, are used to writing in a manner that is short and direct and rarely takes into consideration their own involvement in the situation to which they are referring. It therefore takes more time to help them to develop their reflexive writing" (Rebolledo, personal communication, 2011).

Rebolledo (2011) went on to suggest that, because we live in a very polarized society, students may be hesitant to share their inner reflexions to "share the flow of energy of compassion" and to develop a space within their work world where personal growth can be tackled as directly as professional

Action Research for Business, Nonprofit, and Public Administration

growth. In order to maximize the transformational potential of AR, we must be willing to merge the personal and the professional.

What Do Students Say?

To delve deeper into the student perspective and access the wisdom of people who have traveled the same path as the readers of this book, we asked students to reflect on their AR projects. Some of their comments are included here as just a small glimpse into the thoughts of other action researchers such as yourselves.

Struggles and Difficulties

Three things emerge as general topics when students discussed the challenges they faced and, for the most part, overcame while doing AR. Meeting academic and IRB standards were the biggest challenges, not surprising since this catapults students into the research environment with its own peculiar rules.

- I hated having to start over when my IRB was not allowed due to lack of permission from the agency where I work.

- Realizing that the research study I had written up for a qualitative class was not AR, I had to start over.

- You need to allot more time than you think at the end for data analysis. I had to rush at the end because I didn't realize it was more than just writing my standard report.

The second-most reported struggles dealt with being honest with themselves in reflective and reflexive practice.

- It is hard to be honestly reflexive and reflective. It takes practice to dig deep enough to uncover the flaws in logic or to find the evidence that goes against what is seen on the surface.

Looking back from the end of their studies, students wondered if they could have approached their work from different angles and been able to learn more or go deeper into their issues, ultimately asking, "How could I have anticipated that?" Our students asked this among other things:

- How do I know at the beginning if the project is worth doing or if it will turn out to be good AR?

- How can I anticipate the unexpected from the survey or interview participants?

- Can you use participatory research on just about any project?

We feel as though these get to the central issues of AR as a personal endeavor—the necessity for people in the trenches doing the work to follow their own hearts and roll with the unexpected experiences that come along. To some extent, we can't know whether our projects will hold up, or our interviews will give us the kind of data we expect, or whether a group will be a better way to work than as an individual. Our unanswered questions always take us the next step in our own practice and our understanding of the process.

Lessons Learned and Transformative Qualities

Most students also commented on the positive things that they took away from their experience with AR. They talked about the lessons learned and the positive transformations that had taken place.

The action of putting together a project and being held responsible to measurement and to ongoing reflective and reflexive protocol taught students the value of all the parts of AR. They commented that, when they didn't know what to do next, comments from colleagues, professors, and the use of a process-oriented book helped fill in the gaps of their understanding. Nevertheless, nothing compared to lessons learned just by doing it:

- Trial and error taught me the most.

- The whole AR project was very beneficial. Previous classes like qual and quant were all theory to me, but this class gave me some hands-on experience, which is the way I learn best.

- I saw the whole picture and now know what it takes to do a larger project. This mini project was a great tool to show me where I need to do better and plan more effectively.

In many ways, AR combines the best parts of research and project management. It also can be said that, at the same time, it creates twice the challenge—causing students to confront their own personal assumptions, their time management issues, as well as the ins and outs of research. Some of our readers may identify with the following:

- There are ups and downs to the process. On Monday, I was elated, then Wednesday rolled around, and it was like I was sitting there listening to the tick of the clock wondering if the data I needed would ever come in. Next time, I will prepare better for data collection traumas.

- I learned to plan, reflect, and expect the unanticipated. Next time, I will spend more time in reflection and be more careful in crafting my instruments.

- I learned the difference between analyzing data and using it—I was used to using data and the way I reported it to prove my assumptions. At first, I didn't put enough energy into looking at the evidence that showed other ways of thinking about our problems.

- I learned that you don't have to have a supportive corporate setting to do AR.

- One of my lessons learned was that AR is not about imposing a solution on others.

- The flexibility of AR that allowed my project to be focused on my family life taught me a lot about its flexibility. I now know I can use it in any environment.

- I now understand the difference between just asking the question and trying to do something differently about an issue I face. AR allows me to do both, and I love it.

PAR efforts with teambuilding and team processes led to its own type of learning.

- The major discovery for the past couple of weeks was one of leadership. I had to identify this situation and lead everyone back to the project goal. We discovered that a PAR project has to have someone who keeps the faith and refocuses the team when necessary.

Students always have amazing reflective insight into the beauty of AR and what it requires of them when they finish their projects. In big and small ways, AR continues to be experienced by people who do it as a satisfying and transformational process.

- I have had to take a closer look at how I am thinking about situations and to apply the knowledge I am gaining.

- I never thought about using AR in the past, but now I see it as a tool for change.

- It not only transforms your thinking, but it transforms you emotionally and intellectually, therefore transforming my mind in the path of critical thinking.

Research transforms the researcher as much as it makes an impact on the world at large.

- My takeaway here was the power of the AR and PAR process in consulting engagements. I learned a lot about myself from my good and bad experiences of running the project and about both management and research.

- Completing such a project is inherently satisfying.

What Do the Authors Say?

At the end of a book, we are more aware of all the things we didn't say that could have been added. As Albert Einstein is quoted as saying, "The more I learn, the more I realize I don't know." We hope, however, that this practical guide to the doing of AR will augment the many other valuable books on the theory, the reflective learnings, and the depth of the practice that together make up a rich literature on AR. As one of our students just wrote, "When I learn a new skill, I want a cookbook." We hope that we have stayed true to that vision and that you not only use this cookbook but also go out and investigate the critical ideas that will add to your corner of the business, nonprofit, or public administration world.

AR has a long history of helping people improve their lives, their work, or their educational systems. In this time where the whole world is experiencing change on a scale never before imagined, it is a tool that meets those challenges head-on—helping us all move toward life improvement as we go.

E. Alana James

E. Alana is the main writer for this publication. In drawing on her years of experience leading regional and international PAR groups, using virtual networks to enhance AR practice, and refining the ideas she introduced in her first book published by SAGE Publications: *Participatory Action Research for Educational Leadership: Using Data Driven Decision Making to Improve Schools,* E. Alana also independently mentors doctoral students using AR for their dissertations.

She Adds. My own journey with AR continues to grow as I continue to work on systematically capturing my reflexions and reflections. Philosophically, I am a hard-core pragmatist, and I have always been drawn to this work because I fundamentally believe it can change the world. In fact, it already has in so many ways. My own voice in the work adds to the discursive commentary on what we do and how to make it work better. This always includes blending AR with solid mixed methods research practices and breaking down what I see as unnecessary walls between what is perceived as positivistic research practices and our more democratic view of research.

The challenges faced in the global community today are perhaps literally earth shattering, and AR is the tool that can help people overcome the lethargy that may accompany those facing daunting issues. I invite other AR practitioners to join me in a meta-analysis of what we have already learned as shown in the AR literature. The aim of this project is to ferret out the best practices in our fields along with the theoretical and philosophical perspectives with which AR literature abounds. I join with Kemmis in a call to those using AR to go deeper and wider in our practice to critically debate how, where, and when our efforts can strategically improve our world(s). Together, our work represents a critical view of issues that our projects address, and if we band together to expand our voices, we may help our politicians build flexible structures within policies to be inclusive and address everyone's needs.

Tracesea Slater
Tracesea is the practical arm of the writing team for this volume. As a college and university instructor, she acted as the watchdog that the discussion stayed both accessible and on a practical level.

She Adds. I have personally experienced the transformative power of AR in my own life, and I have seen it transform the lives of others. I have also been witness to the possibilities for change, improvement, and inclusion that AR can bring to organizations. Like many other people in the world today, I know of (and have worked for) many businesses, nonprofits, and other organizations that were in desperate need of improvement in one way or another. As workers, and even as people in positions of authority, we often find ourselves feeling powerless to investigate and create the changes that are clearly needed. We may complain with our coworkers, make futile individual efforts to affect change, or even throw up our hands in despair. It doesn't have to be this way. It is my sincere belief that AR and particularly PAR can effectively be employed in most of these situations to effectively improve many aspects of our working world today.

Besides the power and pragmatism of AR, I am also attracted to its emancipatory and democratizing potentials. There are many other methods for studying problems and creating change in an organization. However, many of these employ a narrow approach that produces a temporary, shortsighted fix that is to the benefit of some at the expense of others. With a PAR approach, the voices and experiences of many can create better and more varied solutions. In addition, PAR can increase the sense of empowerment and cohesion in an organization. PAR can create a win-win situation for an organization, its employees, the populations it serves, and the larger community. That's powerful!

I know that AR works. Participating in an AR project can help an individual develop a lifelong method for analyzing and dealing with issues both personal and professional. The basic process, when broken down, can be so simple, yet it can be used on the most complex of problems. As our lives, our world, our businesses and organizations become increasingly complex, I believe that methods like AR, which incorporate flexibility, inclusion, and reflection, will be the most useful for researching problems and successfully incorporating positive change. It is my sincere hope that this book will allow you to experience the power and potential of the AR process in your own life and that you will spread this potential to others through the businesses and organizations you work with.

Alan Bucknam

Alan brings the visual expertise to this team that created the look and feel of the book, making its contents quickly accessible to our readers. He is also author of all the illustrations.

He Adds. Trial and error has always been an important part of my learning and creative process. In my design practice, when I am working with clients and their stakeholders (both internal and external), utilizing iterative PAR cycles lets us work together to get the best outcome for everyone involved, allowing deeper, more meaningful (and measurable) input from all sides, and producing more effective results. As with the best processes, PAR is scalable, allowing for different scales of time, effort, resources, and scope. This lets me use it on both small and large projects to great effect. Simply put, it serves as an effective tool for improving internal business practices and for managing external outcomes.

The Road Forward

It is tempting to paraphrase Star Trek's "live long and prosper" message as we conclude our book. This finishes what we intended to be the practical arm to balance the theoretical body of literature surrounding AR methodology. The specific focus of this volume on business, nonprofits, and public administration is dedicated to Alana's students at Colorado Technical University and the wealth of information about their worlds, which she has shared with them on their first AR journeys. We close hoping that this same journey is as exciting for

you, our reader, and for all the other students who
come after you as it has been, and remains, for us.

Additional Readings

Baiocchi, G., Heller, P., & Silva, M. K. (2008). Making
space for civil society: Institutional reforms and local
democracy in Brazil. *Social Forces, 86,* 911–936.

Calderon, J. Z., Foster, S., & Rodriquez, S. (2003).
*Organizing immigrant workers: Action research
and strategies in the Pomona day labor center.* Paper
presented at the Annual Meeting of the American
Sociological Association, Atlanta, GA, USA.

Cann, A. P., MacEachen, E., & Vandervoort, A.
A. (2008). Lay versus expert understandings of
workplace risk in the food service industry:
A multi-dimensional model with implications for
participatory ergonomics. *Work, 30,* 219–228.

Sackmann, S. A., Eggenhofer-Rehart, P. M., &
Firesl, M. (2009). Sustainable change: Long-term
efforts toward developing a learning organization.
The Journal of Applied Behavioral Science, 45(4),
521–549.

Appendix A.
Action Research
Proposal Outline

Abstract

Formulate a one-sentence answer for each question, and then combine them into one paragraph.

1. What is the purpose of your research?

2. What is the context of this problem?

3. What is the scope of this research? How many people, departments, and so on, will be measured or affected?

4. How many AR cycles of discovery, measurable action, and reflection were included?

5. What research questions do you hope to answer?

6. What outcomes do you hope to effect with your actions?

7. Who are the stakeholders for your project?

8. What limitations exist?

9. What contribution do you expect this research to make to yourself, your company, and your field?

Action Research Proposal

Background

Write two to three paragraphs on the context of the problem. Include literature citations as appropriate. Back up your ideas whenever possible with data. Cite and reference all data sources.

Local Context

Write two to three paragraphs explaining the local context. Help the reader understand the issues as experienced locally, as well as the importance of the research. Back up the explanations with citations and references from the literature. Use data to quantify your ideas, and cite and reference data sources.

Personal Context

Write two to six paragraphs describing your relationship to and part in this research. Answer the following questions:

1. What is your relationship to the organization where you will be conducting the research?

2. What permissions are needed for data collection and analysis? From whom do you need to get permission? Have you already collected those permissions?

3. Will the change you hope to effect be better served with the ongoing support of a team? If so, will you be gathering a team to conduct PAR? If so, describe the composition of your team, their

roles, how often they will meet, and a timeline for the completion of the project.

4. Describe your personal history in relation to the issue you will be studying and, if a PAR project, your personal history with the other participants.

Gaps in Knowledge

Describe the gaps you hope this research will fill in your local context:

1. What gaps in knowledge exist?

2. What gaps in activity exist between knowledge and action?

Research Questions

List one to four questions you would like to begin to answer:

1. What new information is needed?

2. What new data is needed?

3. What new types of actions are needed?

Research Methodology

Insert a beginning paragraph about the proven efficacy of AR, and then answer the following questions under subheadings relating to each step in the cycle. Each section will likely be three to eight paragraphs with citations and references from the literature, data from your local context, and explanations as appropriate.

Discovery

1. What discovery questions do you need answered prior to taking action toward your desired outcomes?

   a. What data will be examined?

2. What research will be needed, and what tools will be used?

   a. What other sources of data may be required, and how will they be gathered?

Measurable Actions

1. Describe the purpose of your measurable actions.

   a. What do you hope to accomplish? (To what extent does this accomplishment need to impact humans?)

2. What archival data exists, and how will you secure access or permission to use it?

3. What baseline data is needed, how do you plan to gather it, and from whom?

4. What stakeholders will need to be considered?

   a. What forms of data will be most convincing to them?

5. Will there be a population from whom you may have to collect data in order to show relative

efficacy of your action steps? If so, how will you take steps to include a representative sample?

a. Who, if anyone, will be employed to help determine the efficacy of your data collection and analysis of your action steps?

Reflection

1. Describe your reflective tools.

a. How often and under what circumstances will you employ them?

2. Who, if anyone, will be employed to help determine the efficacy of your reflections?

3. How will you record the cycles and your determination of next steps?

Ethical Assurances

1. Who will be included as subjects?

2. In what manner will their data be gathered and recorded?

3. How will you ensure confidentiality of their responses?

4. How will you ensure the safety of your data?

5. What are the risks and benefits to the subjects for participation in your research?

Procedures

Write a paragraph introduction.

Create a timeline. (Complete a table with as many steps as you imagine.)

Description of Steps Needed to Complete Research Project	Due Date

Expected Results

1. What do you hope to accomplish?

2. How many cycles of AR do you anticipate engaging in?

Discussion

This section is used to convince your reader that your expected results are reasonable. Back up the previous section with a short discussion from research literature, literature on the issue you are studying, or on AR literature.

Budget

If there are any budgetary considerations that will need to be addressed as part of this research, write them here; if not, then you can delete this section.

Publication of Results

Who will have publishing rights to any final report that would result from this research? What permissions would be needed within your local context, and from whom will you need to secure these permissions? Do you have any concerns regarding these issues?

If working in a PAR team, how will each member of the team ensure efficacy and rigor of the results? Who has content rights? Who has rights of publication?

Follow-On Studies

1. If it is not within your time limitations to fully answer all your research questions, what do you hope to accomplish?

2. What are the remaining questions, and how will you address them? Over what period of time?

References

Include APA-formatted references for all authors, works, and data cited herein.

Appendix B. Example of Student Answers to Proposal Questions

Purpose

- What is your topic?

  Aerospace engineering culture.

- What questions would you like to answer?

  What inclusion factors influence an engineering organization?

  How does a noninclusive aerospace company become more inclusive?

  What value do multicultural engineers have to the organization's stakeholders?

- Which of these questions will you have time to address in your study, and which will need to be placed in the *further studies* section?

  All questions addressed.

- Why are these questions significant?

  To discover new knowledge and reflect on actions needed to produce a desired future.

- What do you want to do, to accomplish?

  Engage those closest based on successes and needs.

- Why might others care about your problem?

  To further growth and success of the organization.

- How do others see the same set of issues or problems? Back up your ideas with literature.

  Others have the same issues and concerns of not being organized in line with demographic changes, thereby limiting growth and performance. Background literature included in IRB.

- Are there larger, overarching questions or issues that affect what you are researching?

  The overreaching issues concern a lack of research on the subject of engineering inclusion.

- What values do you hold that will guide this work?

  I am a stakeholder within an aerospace engineering company faced with an aging, single-culture workforce. My values include sustaining and increasing performance levels concerning the future of domestic engineering resources.

- How are they in line with general AR principles?

  Stakeholder involvement and engaging participants from inside and outside organizational cultures foster various inquiry cycles and various forms of learning that in turn articulate experiential knowing via creative expression and application.

Scope

- What is the context for this work, including the location, the environmental issues, and the industry standards that create the need to study your issue?

  The context for this research includes large, subprime aerospace engineering companies that typically hire from within or strive to use the same breed of technical resources to achieve an industry standard level of performance.

  Local context includes the company that I work for and surrounding companies that oftentimes share the same resources.

  The environmental issues that are relevant here include organizational sameness that is affected by future demographic changes. The uncertainty, including benefits of change, creates a need to study this issue.

- What is the history of the issue in that location?

  The history of this issue is a desire to stay the same or one that lacks inclusion and diversity.

- How many people are involved in the AR project?

  Approximately 11 people.

- What will be their level of involvement?

  Develop into engineering functional teams within their level of expertise, and organize their experiences through group participation.

- What data already exist about the issue in this specific location? Set up the reader's understanding of the baseline from which you are working. For example, are there incident reports or gaps between policy and actions that you can refer to?

  Hiring from within to maintain consistent levels of experience and culture is nothing new to the business market, especially aerospace. Aerospace engineers, unlike many traditional engineering functions, often specialize in particular types of aerospace products, such as commercial aircraft, military fighter jets, spacecraft, and so on (Bureau of Labor Statistics, 2010). This phenomenon has contributed to an insider group of aerospace engineers most familiar with the cyclical trends of resource requirements. Engineers from other technical industries who do not know the aerospace genre are often not considered or do not fit in.

- What population is affected by the issue you are studying, and how will they be involved in your research?

  The population affected include primarily aerospace engineers as stakeholders and other engineering disciplines as outsiders.

- What specific variable(s) will you be trying to measure?

  Success of other diversified aerospace engineering organizations and technical performance.

Methodology—Describing the Action Research

- Will you be undertaking this project as a lone researcher or part of a participatory group?

  Initially as a lone researcher to research the successes of similar companies followed by a participative role.

- If part of a group, who will be the other participants, and what are their stakes in the project?

  Respective engineering functional group leaders and their group participants.

- If PAR, then have you all agreed upon relative issues of working together? Rights of publication? Dissemination of results?

  Yes—including approved consent forms and an approved IRB.

- How often will you meet?

  Scheduled weekly meetings and impromptu sessions.

Discover Phase

- What do you need to learn before you advance to the action steps?

  An understanding of what other engineering companies are successfully doing to diversify their workforces.

- How will the discovery be undertaken, and who will be responsible for what portions of the work (if done in a group)?

  Myself, as the primary researcher.

Measurable Action Phase

- What natural actions make sense for the first cycle of research?

  Understanding of the research actions and learning history.

- How will their outcomes be measured?

  Through data gathering and technical performance.

- What methods of measurement do you imagine using to gather your data? Note: Because of the evolutionary systems within AR methodology, we recommend a wide list of possible methods that can be honed later.

  Develop and identify a data collection procedure and observation as a tool to analyze the data collected by interpreting all symbols and numbers into text. This method will help to understand the phenomena of the study and to draw correlation between cultural differences and performance as a measure.

- What systems do you have in place to ensure accurate data collection?

  Excel database.

Reflection Phase

- What protocols will you use for keeping reflective notes throughout the process? For instance, will you keep an ongoing journal?

  Reflective tools used in this research project include:

  Weekly status, listed as group minutes, will be used to reflect on what was learned as a group from the previous meetings. This weekly status review will occur during my established weekly staff meetings.

  Team interaction recorded and reviewed to determine strengths and weaknesses surrounding the possible integration of multicultural resources.

  Weekly stakeholder reviews will reflect back on team performance. This will occur during my boss's weekly staff meetings.

- How will you gain experience through active observation and reflection at the moment (reflexive practice)?

  A validation meeting designed to review the things that worked and the things that did not work establishes the forum for peer learning and learning to learn. This peer learning process does not teach learning history but rather identifies the history of events realized from most recent program status by recognizing the actions that worked and did not work, thereby supporting collaborative action. Specific presentations to the functional or local engineering community and to the multicultural or cosmopolitan engineering community consisting of quality, cost, and schedule metrics relate to a common understanding of data tools used to measure organizational performance.

- Will notes be taken at all meetings?

  Yes.

- How are these notes to be analyzed later?

  Comparison based on trends, history, and reflection.

  Note: Findings and conclusions are not included in the proposal stage.

Ethical Assurances

- How will the rights of the people you study be protected?

  Signed consent form.

- What are the rights of the people you are working with on a PAR team?

  The right not to participate or stop at any time.

- What are our relationships with both of these groups?

  Insiders and stakeholders.

- How will you ensure confidentiality?

  No names will be used.

- How will your data be protected?

  Single source and password protected. Discarded after the project is complete.

- How will you work to ensure no undue pressure will be exerted by you?

  Strictly voluntary and on casual time.

- What are the options should people decide they do not want to participate?

  Their choice not to participate with no repercussions.

- What assurances do you offer if they decide not to participate regarding the long-term ramifications of that choice?

  Part of the signed consent form.

Assumptions and Limitations

- What assumptions are you making as you start the study?

  To gain more knowledge from the start.

- What biases do you have about either the process or the outcomes you expect?

  That inclusion may be seen as a negative process.

- What do you wish you could do that you will not be able to do?

  Direct team participation.

- How long will your study be, and do you think you will have all the data you need to complete the study as intended? If not, then list the limit of size or time that makes your study possible, if not perfect.

  Expect the study to be 12 weeks long and to gain new knowledge from the start.

- What other important things will you not have time to get to during this project?

  Measurements after making any changes.

Contributions

- What should people be able to do with the new information that will result from your project?

  Apply it to their own organizations.

- How will your AR study contribute to your field?

  As a researcher in a doctorial research program concerning organizational development and change and as a future consultant.

- How will it contribute to your company?

  As support to future organizational enhancements in line with demographic changes.

- How will it contribute to the world?

  By supporting inclusion and diversity (big deal for me and my eternal footprint on earth).

- What are the implications of your work for the future in your field, your community, or your organization?

  Recognizing and embracing the inclusion process—leading to a diverse environment without having to manage it.

Appendix C.
Student Proposal

Table of Contents

Abstract

The purpose of this research is to perform a data review of how engineering companies have been able to diversify from a single culture of resources to a multicultural level. Current aerospace engineering levels revolve around a single culture of limited resources grown within the ranks of midsize aerospace companies. The scope of this research involves engineers, their supervisors, and program management from two commercial and two defense programs within Vought Aircraft, a midsize aerospace company that supports several major aerospace prime companies. Respective engineering functions and support organizations from separate aerospace programs, approximately 80 people, will be involved with this research. Two research cycles, refining methods, data, and interpretation shall reflect knowledge and experiences that support these further actions. The main questions this AR hopes to answer include what factors influence a diverse engineering organization and what the value of cultural differences is to aerospace engineering stakeholders. The effect of this AR hopes to influence a more inclusive aerospace engineering culture. The major inside stakeholders of this project are program management, site management, functional management, and engineers. Time constraint is a realized limitation to this project, but results represent on-point research. The contribution expected from this AR supports effective action consistent with my intentions toward developing and sustaining a more diverse

Action Research for Business, Nonprofit, and Public Administration

engineering community inside the United States while maintaining or improving the level of organizational performance.

Introduction

Background

Traditionally, large subprime aerospace manufacturing companies hire from within the ranks of the industry, using the same breed of technical resources to achieve a consistent, industry-standard level of expertise. This process works similar to an apprentice program where mentoring members of the same culture is the desire, with understudies mentored by the establishment's finest masters to ultimately and purposely serve as their predecessors. This hiring method yields a consistent, nondiverse level of results that serves to be in the best interest of aerospace managers. Airbus of France, holding more than 50% of the world market for passenger aircraft and rival to Boeing Aircraft Company, has an apprentice program in place where the strategy of growing their own engineers is an important factor in preparing for the future (Sampson, 2006). This method maintains a tight reign of people best suited by management to work at and maintain a set standard of knowledge for the company. It is not a diversified workforce offering a multicultural level of experience but rather a purposely developed status quo.

Hiring from within to maintain consistent levels of experience and culture is nothing new to the business market, especially aerospace. Engineers apply the principles of science and mathematics to develop economical solutions to technical issues. Aerospace engineers, unlike many traditional engineering functions, often specialize in a particular type of aerospace product, such as commercial aircraft, military fighter jets, spacecraft, and so on (Bureau of Labor Statistics, 2010). Outsiders or engineers from outside of aerospace are not as vulnerable to cutbacks in defense spending and in governmental research and development that have resulted in significant layoffs of aerospace engineers in the past. This phenomenon has contributed to an insider group of aerospace engineers most familiar with the cyclical trends of resource requirements. Engineers from other technical industries who do not know the aerospace genre have to adapt to fit in. This is similar with respect to engineers and well-educated professional resources from nonaerospace related fields. Thomas Stewart, Harvard Business News (2005), indicated, "Imported talent tends to do less well than home grown talent." Stuart views the current CEO crisis as caused by too many outside hires and that internal succession plans are required to ensure the future success of the company business.

The "Attraction Paradigm" (Byrne, 1971) considers this comfort level by attracting individuals that prefer their own group. Culture characterizes similar ways of thinking and behaving among members of a functional group (Gibson, 2006). This cultural diversity develops into a group allegiance (Pelled, 1996). Diversity within the commercial aircraft industry is a result of these prior theories. This supports Edmonson and

McManus' (2007) theory that "mature theory presents well-developed constructs and models that have been studied over time with increasing precision" (p. 1158). The theoretical perspective used here is an orienting lens for research relating to specific organizational functions.

Local Context

Vought Aircraft Company, located in Dallas, Texas, employs about 900 to 1,000 engineers spread out over several commercial and defense-oriented aircraft programs. Vought Aircraft is a major subcontractor to several prime aerospace companies including Boeing, Northrop-Grumman, Gulfstream, Airbus, and several U.S. government agencies. These engineering resources are made up of direct Vought employees and contract engineers who often shift between programs based on budget requirements and program needs. Many of these same engineers tend to move between programs their entire careers, limiting an environment of inclusion. Other aerospace companies have fallen into this scenario and have formed their own tight cultures of professionals that perform as if in a personal business. These professionals are made up of direct company employees and contract engineers or "flexible on-demand staffing" (O'Hanlon, 1999) who rotate between companies. As new contracts cause a surge in the need for resources, managers most familiar with their businesses and the routine people available spur these resource needs. Alternatively, the same resources available for hire will reference similar resources, and inclusion is not the priority.

Personal Context

I am the technical project manager for Vought Aircraft in Dallas, Texas, responsible for all Boeing commercial programs. My organization currently consists of 140 full-time engineers. I perform as a functional manager over 11 organizational teams and as the project leader (reference attached organizational chart). Each organizational lead has a team leader who reports directly to me. I am responsible for hiring and professionally nourishing personnel in my organization and usually seek resources from the same company pool of engineers or based on recommendations from insiders or those resources who I believe will fit into the current organizational structure.

Using the current resources within the organization, my plan is to identify teams using my respective team leaders from within the respective functions and conduct PAR. This plan will allow equal participation and individual voices within each team to be used to support this research project.

Problem Statement

I want to investigate concerns about what perceptions surround the reasoning behind choosing/hiring a single versus diverse culture of aerospace engineers, especially when knowing that the current majority source of human resources will soon be the minority.

Purpose Statement

The purpose of this research is to conduct PAR to determine the value of cultural engineering

Action Research for Business, Nonprofit, and Public Administration

differences as a first step in making improvements within the organization.

Research Questions

1. What are the factors that influence a diverse engineering organization?

2. How does a noninclusive aerospace company become more inclusive?

3. What is the value of multicultural engineers to aerospace engineering stakeholders?

Research Design

PAR, having the proven capacity to produce change and effect, is the main research tool used in this research project. This systematic form of inquiry, which is collective, collaborative, self-reflective, critical, and useful by participants of the research (McCutcheon & Jung, 1990), serves as the obvious choice to organize life experiences through group participation.

PAR is important to research as it relates to the individual and cultural level. This method orients approaches to new learning and new knowledge. AR adapts to many audiences through engagement and participation. Multiple audiences recognize the voices of practitioners used to explore and test new ideas and methods. This social dimension allows the research to take place in real-world situations and aims to solve real problems. AR is learning by doing with a prime purpose of turning people involved into researchers.

Discovery

There is a need to discover an understanding of what other engineering companies are doing or what is used by other organizations that have successfully diversified their workforces. Another item for discovery is to determine what others believe is the value of having a multicultural engineering workforce in other applications besides aerospace. Examples of such related discovery may include major aerospace companies that have higher diversity ratings than smaller companies. As an active leader in networking between other programs within my company and as a known manager and leader amongst other aerospace engineering companies within the Dallas and Fort Worth areas, this level of discovery will take minimal effort on my part. Other examples of discovery may also include professional organizations recognized as being diverse, including hospitals, universities, and the tourist industry. This discovery is necessary prior to taking measurable actions.

Measurable Actions

Measurable actions are required to determine the performance level of a more diversified engineering function. To measure these actions, my research will compare the performance levels of more diversified engineering functions and how they relate to my organization. The types of actions here include gathering data from other local aerospace engineering companies and other companies with successful experience in diversity. This data may be publicly available if the company performs work for the government; otherwise, survey data will be obtained as required to lead to this goal of how to measure actions.

To gain a wider perspective of information, it is necessary to use data collection procedures and observation as tools to analyze the data collected by interpreting all symbols and numbers into text. This method will help me to understand the phenomena of my study and to draw correlations between cultural differences and performance as a measure.

Reflection

Reflective tools used in this research project include the following:

- Weekly status, listed as group minutes, will be used to reflect on what was learned as a group from the previous meetings. This weekly status review will occur during my established weekly staff meetings.

- Team interaction will be recorded and reviewed to determine strengths and weaknesses surrounding the possible integration of multicultural resources.

- Weekly stakeholder reviews will reflect back on team performance. This will occur during my boss's weekly staff meetings.

A validation meeting designed to review the things that worked and the things that did not work establishes the forum for peer learning and learning to learn. This peer learning process does not teach learning history but rather identifies the history of events realized from the most recent program status by recognizing the actions that worked and did not work, thereby supporting collaborative action. Specific presentations to the functional or local engineering community and to the multicultural or cosmopolitan engineering community consisting of quality, cost, and schedule metrics relate to a common understanding of data tools used to measure organizational performance.

Data Collection and Analysis

Data Source	Human Subjects/How They Will Be Recruited/Their Work Relationship With You	Type of Analysis
Major aerospace companies within the Dallas/Fort Worth area of the U.S.	Engineers Managers Recruited as part of a focus group and by interviews Coworkers, peers, stakeholders	Reflective learning Learning history PAR Qualitative surveys

Ethical Assurance

Aerospace engineers, the aerospace engineering function, and associated stakeholders, outside of my organization, are subjects of this research project. Data gathered based on focus groups, interviews, and anonymous surveys shall serve managing stakeholders. Individual consent forms shall be obtained by all participating in this research project. Proper IRB requirements shall be verified prior to proceeding.

Procedures

Timeline

Description of Steps Needed to Complete Research Project	Due Date
Define research proposal	4-12-2010
Identify stakeholders	4-26-2010
Identify working teams	5-03-2010
Perform interviews	5-17-2010
Review data	6-07-2010

Expected Results

The overall expectations from this research project are an understanding of the value of cultural differences within an engineering organization and an approach to implement a more inclusive engineering organization. Regardless of the value determined by cultural difference, the majority population of human resources is shifting, as the current majority soon becomes the minority. Ultimately, companies must recognize this shift in resources available. The expected results are for aerospace engineering stakeholders to be more prepared.

The expectations I hope to derive from my AR model is depth and detailed data, vivid and nuanced answers, and an overall richness in responses. Notes and other information will be formulated immediately following each interview and tabulated in spreadsheet format. Broad patterns will be identified and data analyzed using Creswell's (2008) interpretation steps. I anticipate engaging in a minimum of two cycles of AR as time permits.

Discussion

Management focus on local workplace diversity has many U.S. companies looking for ways to include cultural value in their workforce. According to data from the U.S. Census Bureau News (2008) by mid century, current minorities, about one third of the U.S. population, is expected to become the majority in 2042. The current national majority will be 54% minorities in 2050 (U.S. Census Bureau News, 2008). Many companies have initiated plans to explore and implement a more multicultural workplace, while others still rely on the existing and well-established work culture that has sustained their endeavors for several decades. Considering this shift in upcoming resources, aerospace engineering stakeholders must understand the inclusion factors that will lead them into the future.

Budget

The budgetary considerations that need to be addressed as part of this research project are minimal. Casual time (nonpaid company time) is required for those supporting this research during business hours and is included as part of the existing salary process.

Publication of Results

Final publication rights concerning this research project reside exclusively with the research author. A verbal disclaimer shall be made with each contributor to the research in accordance with IRB requirements. Stakeholders within the PAR team shall receive a completed report.

Follow-On Studies

This research proposal serves to accomplish further data needed to support a comprehensive research project. Collaboration, using second person action and reflection, will involve the participation and empowerment of outsider partners to exchange the new knowledge across other groups. Engaging participants working together from inside and outside a culture or project provides an inquiring group of coresearchers and cosubjects. This participation of stakeholders and process owners to research cultural knowledge is an appropriate way to explore new knowledge. Innovative methods to cocreate knowledge include cooperative inquiry and related forms of participative research. Inquiry cycles of action and reflection determine how we know what we do not know. Various ways of knowing contribute to the quality of learning and to this cycle of inquiry. Experiential learning is a quality associated with openness and awareness to surroundings. This quality is knowing through relationships and direct association with people, places, and things (Reason & Bradbury, 2007). Presentational leaning is a quality of knowledge that articulates experiential knowing in a creative manner. This quality of knowing through relational stories provides a level of creative expression. Propositional knowing is a quality of intellectual knowledge. This quality relates to the specific and clear thinking path of proven acceptance. Finally, the practical knowing researched here is a quality that focuses on cultural practices. This quality relates to knowing how to do something using the interpersonal talents of an individual or culture.

The remaining questions will be addressed through forum presentations and professor feedback during the second quarter of 2010.

References

Bureau of Labor Statistics. (2010). *Occupational Outlook Handbook, 2010–11 Edition, Engineers.* U.S. Department of Labor. Retrieved April 21, 2010, from http://www.bls.gov/oco/ocos027.htm

Byrne, D. (1971). *The attraction paradigm.* New York: Academic Press.

Creswell, J. W. (2008). *Educational research: planning, conducting, and evaluating Quantitative and qualitative research* (3rd ed.). Upper Saddle River, NJ: Pearson Education, Inc.

Gibson, C. (2006). Unpacking the concept of virtuality: The effects of geographic dispersion, electronic dependence, dynamic structure, and national diversity on team innovation. *Administrative Science Quarterly. 51*(3), 451–495.

McCutcheon, G. & Jung, B. (1990). Alternative perspectives on action research. *Theory into practice, 29*(3), 144–151.

O'Hanlon, C. (1999). Finders keepers. *American Printer, 223*(5), 26–29.

Pelled, L. (1996). Demographic diversity, conflict and work group outcomes: An intervening process theory. *Organization Science. 7,* 615–631.

Reason, P, & Bradbury, H. (2008). *Handbook of action research: Participative inquiry and practice* (2nd ed.). London: Sage.

Sampson, B. (2006). Grow your own engineers. *Professional Engineering, 19*(5), 25.

Stewart, T. (2005). Picking and choosing. *Harvard Business Review, 83*(2), 10.

U.S. Census Bureau News. (2008). *An older and more diverse nation by midcentury.* Retrieved April 9, 2010, from http://www.census.gov/ Press Release/www/releases/archives/pop

Appendix D.
Action Research
Weekly Report

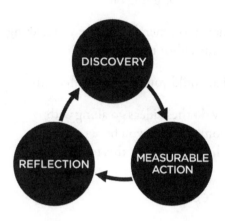

Weekly Report: Name and Title of What Is Being Researched

Discovery

- What happened this week?

- What did you learn from it?

- How did these new ideas change the way you are thinking or taking action?

Measurable Action

- What is your baseline?

- What steps have you taken?

- Has it improved?

- Where are you on the scale from where you started to where you want to go?

Reflection
- What do you think or feel about what is going on?

- What recommendations are you making to yourself for the next cycle?

- What could you be doing differently?

- How do these ideas go along with or contrast what you have read in the literature about this topic?

Next Steps

Appendix E.
Table for Measurable Actions

Date	Baseline	Action	Measurement	Outcome

Appendix F.
Year-Long Guide
for Networked
Action Research

This design is an example of a year-long process to implement strategic change across either several departments or a geographically diverse organization. It was implemented first over a 5-year period of time across several states as more than 30 schools sought to change their practices to improve the education of homeless children and youth, and it has proven efficacy (James, 2006b, 2007, 2009; James et al., 2008).

What follows is the luxury edition of this design, and it includes all the possible support systems that will ensure success. Because of the expense involved in time and resources, this would likely be undertaken by governmental agencies or multinational firms. Still, it is instructive as to what the ideal is, and from it, students may pair down to what is within their scope.

For this complete facilitation pattern, there are three types of participation: (1) the facilitator who leads the meetings and is ultimately responsible to the stakeholders for the success of the process, (2) the facilitators in training, a group of people chosen to learn the process in the first year so that they can lead it in subsequent years, allowing it to become systemic within the organization, and (3) the participants who do the work, come regularly to the group meetings, and who, as part of local teams, are responsible to write reports at the end of their research, outcomes, and findings.

The setup below is broken out into a facilitated set of meetings over the course of 9 months, and participants include directors and staff from the organization in the local teams, the facilitators in training, and the consultant.

During and After the First Meeting (Beginning of the Project)

1. Articulate the ideals and values that guide their work practices and then critically analyze what constrains them from working toward or actualizing those values. The focus of the rest of the professional development is to embed those pedagogical values in their practice as they pursue the goals of their organization.

2. Discuss the goals and objectives given to the project by the organization and what constrains or inhibits the immediate successful completion of those goals.

3. Discuss communication protocols for the group between meetings, including but not limited to, brief weekly reflections on the project sent by e-mail to the facilitators in training to be passed on biweekly to the consultant.

4. Set interim goals and objectives as to what they need to discover in their first round of networked action research (NAR) activity and how they will accomplish those goals. This ends

Action Research for Business, Nonprofit, and Public Administration

the first NPAR meeting, and the local teams go back to their places, where the local teams work to discover what they can.

During and After the Second Meeting (7 to 8 Weeks Later)

1. The local facilitators in training set up and conduct an interim visit to each place where the local teams work.

2. During their second meeting, the participants discuss what they have discovered. They break into small groups to plan ways and means in which they can change their concrete behaviors to make them consistent with their values, overcome the challenges they face, and meet the objectives of their organizations.

3. The consultant facilitates the ways and means for them to successfully measure the outcomes of their intended actions, and the group sets interim goals for their first measurable action cycle.

4. The second meeting ends with a discussion of the importance of catching reflexions and reflections. Protocols are set for consistency.

5. The local facilitators in training set up and conduct an interim visit to each place where the local teams work to help with the measurable action portion of their work.

6. During the interim between the second and third meeting, the participants collaboratively gather data, and it becomes a self-training

exercise for participants to study and improve their own practice along the lines of the agreed-upon values and ideas.

During and After the Third Meeting (7 to 8 Weeks Later)

1. By the third meeting, the group can see that they are developing a knowledge base of how they recommend to others how to actually implement the aims of their organizations—this throws them into a reflective part of the cycle.

2. The consultant facilitates the ways and means in which deeper reflection and capturing reflexive moments can aid participants in seeing the assumptions they are making and to identify ways in which they can dig deeper into their subjects to build stronger, long-term outcomes.

3. Participants break into critical small groups and plan what they need to discover as they start their second round of research.

4. The consultant facilitates planning for how the projects will continue between meetings, and the facilitators in training set up and later conduct interim visits to each place where the local teams work to help with the that process.

Meetings 4, 5, and 6 Proceed in Much the Same Way as the Earlier Meetings, While at the Same Time:

1. The consultant introduces planning for and execution of the final reports.

Action Research for Business, Nonprofit, and Public Administration

2. Participants learn to and execute the report of data from which to derive specific findings and conclusions that will be helpful to their colleagues in future years who are undergoing the same reform.

3. Facilitators in training complete their own AR processes to help them define their own values and ideals for working with groups, analyzing the issues that make this complex, and developing an implementation plan for the organization they serve that will ensure the project is ongoing and successful over time.

4. The consultant gathers data for the report to the organization as to the success of the project, challenges faced, and recommendations for ongoing success.

Support from the organization is needed to provide the following:

1. The project consultant and two assistants, as needed, to facilitate both the professional development and to train trainers who will facilitate in future years as well as to manage the program and facilitate the writing of the final reports for publication. This work will take place over the course of 9 months to a year.

2. People chosen to be trained as facilitators so that the project can continue after its initial year.

3. Sites chosen as good potential sites for reform. Participants from the places where the local

teams work should be the principals or headmasters, and two or more people who are chosen by them to make up the local teams.

4. Support for a stipend to be given to participants when they complete their final reports. For instance, in Sri Lanka, 5,000 rupees per lecturer are given for each completed AR project and report on their studies. Then, they report back to the organization who publishes these reports by topic to help other directors and staff members or other departments.

5. Support for 8 days of meeting times with the six to eight local teams meeting with the consultant, one of the assistants, and the people chosen to become facilitators the next year.

6. Support for two additional half days surrounding each session, one before and one after the eight meeting days described above. Here, the eight people chosen to be given the opportunity to learn facilitation first debrief what they have seen in support of places where the local teams work between meetings and then subsequently debrief the meeting with the local teams. They also set the agenda for the time between visits and for the next meeting. These people will be asked to stay in touch with the consultant and the assistant through virtual communication between visits.

7. Publishing support for the final reports to include publication costs, copy editing, and binding as well as distribution as desired by the organization.

Appendix G.
Model Informed Consent

Research Description

Description of the Research

As a participant in the (name of study and name of university) on the (topic of study) you are being asked to partake in (type of data collection) to confirm, amend, or deny (what kind of information) as to (the goal or purpose of the AR research project). Data collected from you in the form of (list forms of data) will be for the purposes of either addressing the following questions or issues:

1. Issue on which the study is based

2. Research question 1

3. Research question 2

4. And so on

Participants
You are being asked to participate in the study because . . . .

Procedures
Your voluntary participation in this study will entail . . . .

Benefits of Participation
There (may or may not) be direct benefits to you as a participant in this study. However, the aim of the

project is to learn . . . and the benefits of the project long term should be . . . .

Risks of Participation

There are risks involved in all research studies. This study may include only minimal risks. State the level of anticipated risks (i.e., you may become uncomfortable or feel embarrassed when answering some questions).

Compensation

This study is likely to take up . . . of your time for which you will receive . . . level of compensation (no compensation is normal).

Contact Information

If you have any questions or concerns about the study, you may contact (list your professor), and you should know that you can easily withdraw your participation at any time by also calling that number.

Voluntary Participation

Your participation in this study is voluntary. You may refuse to participate in this study or in any part of this study with no harm to you or our relationship. You may withdraw at any time without prejudice to any relationships you may have. You are encouraged to ask questions about this study at the beginning or any time during the research study.

Confidentiality

All information gathered in this study will be kept completely confidential. No reference will be made in written or oral materials that could link you to

Action Research for Business, Nonprofit, and Public Administration

this study. All records will be stored in a locked facility at least 3 years after completion of the study. After the storage time, the information gathered will be . . . . Data will be aggregated, and all identifying remarks will be removed prior to publication unless I contact you to ask permission to quote you.

Participant Consent

I have read the above information and agree to participate in this study. I am at least 18 years of age. A copy of this form has been given to me.

Signature of Participant _____   Date _____

Participant Name (Please Print) _____

Investigator's Verification of Explanation

I certify that I have carefully explained the purpose and nature of this research to _____
_____ (participant's name) in age-appropriate language. He/She has had the opportunity to discuss it with me in detail. I have answered all his/her questions and he/she provided the affirmative agreement (i.e. assent) to participate in this research.

Investigator's Signature: _____   Date _____

Participant's Rights

Principal Investigator: Emily Alana James

Research Title: A Study of the Use of Participatory Action Research to Create New Educational Practices for Homeless and Highly Mobile Students

I have read and discussed the Research Description with the researcher. I have had the opportunity to ask questions about the purposes and procedures regarding this study.

- My participation in this research is voluntary. I may refuse to participate or withdraw from participation at any time without jeopardy to future medical care, employment, student status, or other entitlements.

- The researcher may withdraw me from the research at his/her professional discretion.

- If, during the course of the study, significant new information that has been developed becomes available that may relate to my willingness to continue to participate, the investigator will provide this information to me.

- Any information derived from the research project that personally identifies me will not be voluntarily released or disclosed without my separate consent, except as specifically required by law.

- If at any time I have any questions regarding the research or my participation, I can contact the investigator, who will answer my questions. The investigator's phone number is (303) 860-1705.

- If at any time I have comments or concerns regarding the conduct of the research or questions about my rights as a research subject, I should contact the Teachers College, Columbia University Institutional Review Board /IRB. The phone number for the IRB is (212) 678-4105. Or, I can write to the IRB at Teachers College, Columbia University, 525 W. 120th Street, New York, NY, 10027, Box 151.

- I should receive a copy of the Research Description and this Participant's Rights document.

- If video and/or audio taping is part of this research, I ( ) consent to be audio/videotaped. I ( ) do NOT consent to being video/audio taped. The written, video and/or audio taped materials will be viewed only by the principal investigator and members of the research team.

- Written, video and/or audio taped materials ( ) may/ ( ) may NOT be viewed in an educational setting outside the research

- My signature means that I agree to participate in this study.

Participant's signature: _____   Date:____/____/____

Name: _____

Investigator's Verification of Explanation

I certify that I have carefully explained the purpose and nature of this research to _____
_____ (participant's name) in age-appropriate language. He/She has had the opportunity to discuss it with me in detail. I have answered all his/her questions and he/she provided the affirmative agreement (i.e., assent) to participate in this research.

Investigator's Signature: _____ Date: _____

Action Research for Business, Nonprofit, and Public Administration

Glossary of Terms

Action research (AR)—a three-stage, iterative methodological process that aims to create positive change while measuring results. It has been shown to be transformative for the researcher as well as the situation under study and is therefore also used for professional development purposes.

Action learning (AL)—ongoing processes that propel an organization to embed learning throughout its processes and structures. Using protocols that enhance learning, AL focuses on critical analysis of situations.

Action learning action research (ALAR)—where researchers manage the projects that they simultaneously study.

Action science (AS)—develops processes and circumstances to aid organizational development and overcome barriers to change. Communities of inquiry develop theories of action and then test their understanding in an iterative process.

Appreciative inquiry (AI)—coevolutionary research aimed at finding the best in situations and building toward a positive future.

Assumptions and limitations—the personal and contextual issues that may limit the credibility, validity, or reliability of a study.

Authenticity—developed by Guba and Lincoln (1986) as an alternative to credible, valid, and reliable measures, especially geared toward evaluation research. Four subtopics are discussed: fairness, ontological authenticity, educative authenticity, and catalytic authenticity.

Beneficence and nonmalfeasance—the ethical stance in research to do no harm.

Community-based participatory research (CBPR)—used primarily in health care, this methodology asks the wider community to engage in an equitable manner with health care providers as they study health disparities.

Conclusions—what the author of the study derives from his or her findings as they impact their lives, their contexts, and the industries or work environments involved.

Contributions—what the study adds to the context or literature in which it is embedded.

Credibility—whether and to what extent AR findings are believable to others.

Emancipatory research—an ideal frequently identified with AR where the people engaged reach beyond their current circumstances and address the power situations inherent in the current reality. They are able to move beyond those constraints to a new reality that contains a greater level of democracy, equitable action, and inclusiveness.

Fidelity and responsibility—the ethical stance in research that the work will promote trust through its benefit to the context and community in which it is embedded.

Findings—the outcomes of data as analyzed to answer the questions and purposes that drive the study.

Hub and spoke—a pattern of communication and activity useful to NPAR where people engaged at a distance in a project (the spokes) come together to confer and share learning (meeting in the hub). Periodic communication unites hub and spoke activity into a fast-paced and potentially transformative potential as it makes use of both the power of weak ties and of many hands making light work.

Insider research—when a researcher studies his or her place of employment or a group in which he or she is normally an active participant.

Justice—the ethical stance in research that all persons will have equal access and benefit from the study and that none are held back due to bias or prejudice.

Ladder of inference—developed out of Argyris's work on defensiveness, the ladder of inference reminds us that, when we hear a comment, we infer more than what may have been meant by the other person. We tend to act from that inference, which may propel unnecessary misunderstandings or conflict.

Living theory—using reflection and reflexion during AR to aid the researcher in reaching his or her highest ideals.

Methods—the tools of research: qualitative and quantitative or mixtures of both in data collection and analysis.

Methodology—the overarching ideas that tie the actions taken to collect and analyze data together.

Networked participatory action research (NPAR)—groups of people either working in proximity or across virtual realities on a similar project or issue. Participants may or may not have similar roles, but they employ the power of group dynamics to ferment activity over time to create positive change.

Participatory action learning action research (PALAR)—as per Zuber-Skerritt (2011), PALAR merges self-directed learning, AR, and leadership.

Participatory action research (PAR)—brings the power of diverse people to engage together in an inclusive and equitable manner to complete an AR project.

Purpose—the underlying reason or motivation behind a research study. Usually, this term is used in qualitative methodologies.

Reliability—demonstration that the results of AR demonstrate one-to-one correlation of data to findings, could be applicable to other settings, and make use of the voice of diverse populations within their study.

Respect for people's rights and dignity—the ethical stance in research to be aware of; that is, to respect and promote the dignity of all persons.

Scope—explains the context for the study in quantifiable terms as it defines the size of the populations and the variables under consideration.

Sensemaking—according to Weick (2009), it is the ongoing retrospective development of plausible stories and images that explain and rationalize what people have done.

Trustworthiness—developed by Guba and Lincoln (1986) as an alternative to credible, valid, and reliable measures, especially geared toward evaluation research. It's a measure of whether the research demonstrates value, applicability, consistency and neutrality.

Validity—whether and to what extent AR demonstrates the ability to increase personal and community knowledge and results in improvement.

Weak tie—when useful information is passed through relatively weak networked connections that our closer and more intimate relationships would be unable to know or share.

References

Anderson, G. L., Herr, K., & Nihlen, A. S. (2005). *Studying your own school: An educator's guide to qualitative practitioner research.* Thousand Oaks, CA: Corwin.

Anonymous Reviewer. (2011). *Peer review of action research for business, nonprofits, and public administration: A tool for complex times during production.* Unpublished book review.

Argyris, C. (1990). *Overcoming organizational defenses. Facilitating organizational learning.* Boston: Allyn and Bacon.

Argyris, C. (2002a). Double-loop learning, teaching and research. *Academy of Management Learning and Education, 1*(2), 206.

Argyris, C. (2002b). Teaching smart people how to learn. *Reflections (1524–1734), 4*(2), 4.

Argyris, C., Putnam, R., & Smith, D. M. (1985). *Action science.* San Francisco: Jossey-Bass.

Argyris, C., & Schön, D. A. (1974). *Theory in practice: Increasing professional effectiveness.* San Francisco: Jossey-Bass Publishers.

Argyris, C., & Schön, D. A. (1978). *Organizational learning.* Reading, MA: Addison-Wesley.

Attwater, R., & Derry, C. (2005). Engaging communities of practice for risk communication in the Hawkesbury Water recycling scheme. *Action Research, 3*(2), 193–209.

Barabasi, A. L. (2002). *Linked: The new science of networks.* New York: Perseus.

Barabasi, A. L. (2005). Network theory-the emergence of the creative enterprise. *Science, 308*(29), 639–642. Retrieved April 11, 2010, from http://www.scribd.com/doc/7794141/Network-Theory-the-Emergence-of-the-Creative-Enterprise

Bate, P. (2000). Synthesizing research and practice: Using the action research approach in health care settings. *Social Policy & Administration, 34*(4), 478–493.

Bawden, R., & Zuber-Skerritt, O. (2002). The concept of process management. *The Learning Organization, 9*(3), 132–138.

Beins, B. C. (2004). *Research methods: A tool for life.* Boston: Pearson.

Benn, S., & Dunphy, D. (2008). Action research as an approach to integrating sustainability into MBA Programs: An exploratory study. *Journal of Management Education, 33*(3), 276–295.

Baiocchi, G., Heller, P., & Silva, M. K. (2008). Making space for civil society: Institutional reforms and local democracy in Brazil. *Social Forces, 86,* 911–936.

Bens, I. (2008). *Facilitation at a glance!* Salem, NH: Goal QPC.

Bradbury, H., Mirvis, P., Neilsen, E., & Pasmore, W. (2008). Action research at work: Creating the future following the path from Lewin. In P. Reason & H. Bradbury (Eds.), *The SAGE handbook of action research: Participative inquiry and practice* (2nd ed., pp. 77–92). London: Sage.

Brannick, T., & Coghlan, D. (2007). In defense of being "native": The case for insider academic research. *Organizational Research Methods, 10*(1), 59–74.

Brause, R. S. (2000). *Writing your doctoral dissertation: Invisible rules for success.* London: Routledge Falmer.

Brent, D. (2006). Complexity and education: Vital simultaneities. *Educational Philosophy and Theory, 40*(1), 50.

Brown, L. D., & Gaventa, J. (2010). Constructing transnational action research networks: Reflections on the Citizenship Development Research Centre. *Action Research, 8*(1), 5–28.

Calderon, J. Z., Foster, S., & Rodriquez, S. (2003). *Organizing immigrant workers: Action research and strategies in the Pomona day labor center.* Paper presented at the Annual Meeting of the American Sociological Association, Atlanta, GA, USA.

Cann, A. P., MacEachen, E., & Vandervoort, A. A. (2008). Lay versus expert understandings of workplace risk in the food service industry: A multi-dimensional model with implications for participatory ergonomics. *Work, 30,* 219–228.

Carter, B. (2010). *Networked PAR in Marion County.* Colorado Springs, CO: Colorado Technical University.

Coghlan, D., & Brannick, T. (2005). *Doing action research in your own organization.* London: Sage.

Coghlan, D., & Coughlan, P. (2006). Designing and implementing collaborative improvement in the extended manufacturing enterprise. *The Learning Organization, 13*(2), 152–165.

Cook, D., Heintzman, L., & McVicker, J. (2004). Three elementary schools' experiences with access to services, welcoming culture and thoughtful placement of students. In E. A. James & M. Milenkiewicz (Eds.), *Colorado Educators Study Homeless and Highly Mobile Students.* Denver, CO: Center for Research Strategies.

Cooperrider, D. L., & Whitney, D. K. (1999). *Appreciative inquiry.* Williston, VT: Berrett Koehler Communications.

Cooperrider, D. L., & Whitney, D. K. (2005). *Appreciative inquiry: A positive revolution in change.* San Francisco: Berrett-Koehler.

Creswell, J. W. (2002). *Educational research: Planning, conducting, and evaluating quantitative and qualitative research.* London: Pearson Education.

Creswell, J. W. (2003). *Research design: Qualitative, quantitative, and mixed method approaches* (2nd ed.). Thousand Oaks, CA: Sage.

Creswell, J. W. (2009). *Research design: Qualitative, quantitative, and mixed methods approaches* (3rd ed.). Thousand Oaks, CA: Sage.

Cunliffe, A. L. (2004). On becoming a critically reflexive practitioner. *Journal of Management Education, 28*(4), 407–426.

Cunliffe, A. L. (2005). The need for reflexivity in public administration. *Administration & Society, 37*(2), 255–242.

Daley, A. (2010). Reflections on reflexivity and critical reflection as critical research practices. *Affilia, 25*(1), 68–82.

Day, C. & Hadfield. (2004). Learning through networks: Trust, partnerships and the power of action research. *Educational Action Research, 12*(4), 575–586.

Day, C. & Townsend, A. (2007). Ethical issues for consultants in complex collaborative action research settings: Tensions and dilemmas. In A. Campbell & S. Groundwater-Smith (Eds.), *An ethical approach to practitioner research: Dealing with issues and dilemmas in action research* (pp. 42–61). London: Routledge.

Day, C., & Townsend A. (2009). Practitioner action research: Building and sustaining success through networked learning communities. In S. E. Noffke & B. Somekh (Eds.), *The SAGE handbook of educational action research* (pp. 178–189). London: Sage

Dorner, D. (1996). *The logic of failure: Recognizing and avoiding error in complex situations.* Cambridge, MA: Perseus Books.

Downey, L. H., Ireson, C. L., & Scutchfield, F. D. (2009). The use of photovoice as a method of facilitative deliberation. *Health Promotion Practice, 10*(3), 419–427.

Doyle, P., & Brannick, T. (2003). Towards developing a food safety model: An insider research approach. *Irish Journal of Management, 24*(2), 38–54.

Drobney, B. (2005). *COPAR paper.* Denver, CO: Colorado Department of Education and the Center for Research Strategies.

Easterling, D., Gallagher, K., & Lodwick, D. G. (2003). *Promoting health at the community level.* Thousand Oaks CA: Sage.

Elliott, J. (1991). *Action research for educational change.* Milton Keynes, England: Open University Press.

Elliott, J. (2006). *Reflecting where the action is: The selected works.* London, New York: Routledge.

Erwin, D. (2009). Changing organizational performance: Examining the change process. *Hospital Topics, 87*(3), 28–40.

Fengning, D. (2009). Building action research teams: A case of struggles and successes. *Journal of Cases in Educational Leadership, 12*(2), 8–18.

Fletcher, M., Zuber-Skerritt, O., Brendan, B., Albertyn, R., & Kearney, J. (2010). Meta-action research on a leadership development program: A process model for life-long learning. *Systemic Practice and Action Research, 23*(6), 487–507.

Fowler, F. J. (2002). *Survey research methods.* Thousand Oaks, CA: Sage.

Freire, P. (2000). *Pedagogy of the oppressed* (30th anniversary ed.). New York: Continuum.

Freire, P., & Freire, A. M. A. (1994). *Pedagogy of hope: Reliving pedagogy of the oppressed.* New York: Continuum.

Friedman, V. J., & Rogers, T. (2008). Action science: Linking causal theory and meaning making in action research In P. Reason & H. Bradbury (Eds.), *The SAGE handbook of action research: Participative inquiry and practice* (2nd ed., pp. 252–265). London: Sage.

Fuller-Rowell, T. E. (2009). Multi-site action research: Conceptualizing a variety of multi-organization practice. *Action Research, 7*(4), 363–384.

Gaventa, J., & Cornwall, A. (2008). Power and knowledge. In P. Reason & H. Bradbury (Eds.), *The SAGE handbook of action research: Participative inquiry and practice* (2nd ed., pp. 172–189). London: Sage.

Glanz, J. (2003). *Action research: An educational leader's guide to school improvement* (2nd ed.). Norwood, MA: Christopher-Gordon Publishers.

Goff, R. (2009). *PAR project.* (AR projects from MGMT 816). Colorado Springs, CO: Colorado Technical University.

Goleman, D. (2006a). *Emotional intelligence* (Bantam 10th anniversary hardcover ed.). New York: Bantam Books.

Goleman, D. (2006b). *Emotional intelligence* (Bantam 10th anniversary hardcover ed.). New York: Bantam Books.

Gorard, S. (2003). *Quantitative methods in social science.* New York, London: Continuum.

Granovetter, M. S. (1995). *Getting a job: A study of contacts and careers* (2nd ed.). Chicago: University of Chicago Press.

Granovetter, M. S., & Swedberg, R. (2011). *The sociology of economic life* (3rd ed.). New York: Perseus Book Group.

Greenwood, D. J., & Levin, M. (1998). *Introduction to action research: Social research for social change.* Thousand Oaks, CA: Sage.

Greenwood, D. J., & Levin, M. (2007). *Introduction to action research: Social research for social change* (2nd ed.). Thousand Oaks, CA: Sage.

Guba, E. G., & Lincoln, Y. S. (1985). *Naturalistic inquiry.* Beverly Hills, CA: Sage.

Guba, E. G., & Lincoln, Y. S. (1986). *But is it rigorous? Trustworthiness and authenticity in naturalistic evaluation* (Vol. 30). San Francisco: Jossey Bass.

Guba, E., & Lincoln, Y. S. (1989). *Fourth generation evaluation.* Thousand Oaks, CA: Sage.

Gustavsen, B., Hansson, A., & Qvale, T. U. (2008). Action research and the challenge of scope. In P. Reason & H. Bradbury (Eds.), *The SAGE handbook of action research: Participative inquiry and practice* (2nd ed., pp. 63–76). London: Sage.

Haslett, T., Barton, J., Stephens, J., Schell, L., & Olsen, J. (2010). Leadership in a network learning: Business action research at Monash University. *The Learning Organization, 17*(1), 104–116.

Hearn, G., Foth, M., & Gray, H. (2009). Applications and implementations of new media in corporate communications. *Corporate Communications: An International Journal, 14*(1), 49–61.

Heifetz, R. A. (2000). *Leadership without easy answers* (2nd ed.). Cambridge, MA: Belnap Press, Harvard University.

Herr, K., & Anderson, G. L. (2005). *The action research dissertation.* Thousand Oaks, CA: Sage.

Hughes, I. (2008). Action research in healthcare. In P. Reason & H. Bradbury (Eds.), *The SAGE handbook of action research: Participative inquiry and practice* (2nd ed., pp. 381–393). London: Sage.

Inglegard, A., Roth, J., Shani, A., & Styhre, A. (2002). Dynamic learning capability and actionable knowledge creation. *The Learning Organization, 9*(2), 65–77.

Jakubik, M. (2008). Experiencing collaborative knowledge creation processes. *The Learning Organization, 15*(1), 5–25.

James, E. A. (2005). Prospects for the future: Use of participatory action research to study issues of educational disadvantage. *Journal of Irish Educational Research, 24*(2–3), 199–206.

James, E. A. (2006a, September). *Implementing a national program for educators to use PAR to study disadvantage: What works?* Paper presented at the ECER 2006, Geneva.

James, E. A. (2006b). A study of PAR for educators developing new practice in areas of educational disadvantage. *Educational Action Research, 14*(4), 525–534.

James, E. A. (2007, 5 September). *Valid to whom and in what way? The transformational potential of Participatory Action Research used as professional development.* Paper presented at the BERA, London.

James, E. A. (2009). *Participatory action research as professional development: Creating new education practices for homeless or highly mobile students in the United States.* Saarbrucken, Germany: VDM Verlag.

James, E. A., Milenkiewicz, M., & Bucknam, A. (2008). *Participatory action research: Data driven decision making for educational leadership.* Thousand Oaks, CA: Sage.

James, P., & Gittins, J. W. (2007). Local landscape character assessment: An evaluation of community-led schemes in Cheshire. *Landscape Research, 32,* 423–442.

Jones, E. (2010). Enhancing professionalism through a professional practice portfolio. *Reflective Practice, 11*(5), 593–605.

Kemmis, S. (2006). Participatory action research and the public sphere. *Educational Action Research, 14*(4), 459–476.

Ketola, T. (2006). Foresight strategies and practices based on regional religious values and global virtue ethics. *Fennia, 184*(1), 27–36.

Keyser, B. (2010). *Action research class project.* (MGMT 816). Colorado Springs, CO: Colorado Technical University.

Kock Jr., N. F., McQueen, R. J., & Corner, J. (1997). The nature of data, information and knowledge exchanges in business processes: implications for process improvement and organizational learning. *The Learning Organization, 4*(2), 70–80.

Laverty, P. (2010). *Action research class project.* (MGMT 816). Colorado Springs, CO: Colorado Technical University.

Lee, C. W. (2007). Is there a place for private conversation in public dialogue? Comparing stakeholder assessments of informal communication in collaborative regional planning. *American Journal of Sociology, 113,* 41–96.

Lewis, J., & Ritchie, J. (2003). Generalizing from qualitative research. In J. Ritchie & J. Lewis (Eds.), *Qualitative research practice.* Thousand Oaks, CA: Sage.

Lincoln, Y. S., & Guba, E. (1989). Ethics: The failure of positivist science. *Review of Higher Education, 12*(3), 221–240.

Ludema, J. D., & Fry, R. E. (2008). The practice of appreciative inquiry. In P. Reason & H. Bradbury (Eds.),

Action Research for Business, Nonprofit, and Public Administration

The SAGE handbook of action research: Participative inquiry and practice (2nd ed., pp. 280–296). London: Sage.

Margolin, I. (2007). Shaping a new professional identity by building a new personal concept of leadership through action research. *Educational Action Research, 15*(4), 519–543.

Martin, A. W. (2008). Action research on a large scale: Issues and practices. In P. Reason & H. Bradbury (Eds.), *The SAGE handbook of action research: Participative inquiry and practice* (2nd ed., pp. 394–406). London: Sage.

Maxwell, J. A. (1996). *Qualitative research design: An interactive approach* (Vol. 41). Thousand Oaks, CA: Sage.

Medaglia, R. (2007). Measuring the diffusion of eParticipation: A survey on Italian local government. *Information Polity: The International Journal of Government & Democracy in the Information Age, 12,* 265–280.

Miller, M. B. M. (2008). Ethics and action research: Deepening our commitment to principles of social justice and redefining systems of democratic practice. In P. Reason & H. Bradbury (Eds.), *The SAGE handbook of action research: Participative inquiry and practice* (2nd ed., pp. 199–210). London: Sage.

Morfitt, Y., & Cox, A. (2008). Motivating norms. In M. Milenkiewicz (Ed.), *Colorado Participatory*

Action Research. Denver Colorado Department of Education.

Mosher, H. (2009). Issues of power in collaborative research with dignity village. *Cultural Studies <=> Critical Methodologies, 10*(1), 43–50.

National College for School Leadership. (2006). Network leadership in action: Getting started with networked collaborative enquiry. *Networked Learning Communities.* Retrieved August 11, 2006, from http://www.nationalcollege.org.uk/index/docinfo.htm?id=133219

Nelson, S. L. (2002). *Excel data analysis for dummies.* Hoboken, NJ: Wiley.

Network, A. S. (2011). Home page. Retrieved April 11, 2011, from http://www.actionscience.com/

Ospina, S., Dodge, J., Gabriella, E., & Hofmann-Pinilla, A. (2008). Taking the action turn: Lessons from bringing participation to qualitative research. In P. Reason & H. Bradbury (Eds.), *The SAGE handbook of action research: Participatory inquiry and practice* (pp. 420–434). London: Sage.

Pace, L. A., & Argona, D. R. (1991). Participatory action research: A view from Xerox. In W. F. Whyte (Ed.), *Participatory action research* (pp. 56–69). Newbury Park, CA: Sage.

Patton, M. Q., & Patton, M. Q. (2002). *Qualitative research and evaluation methods* (3rd ed.). Thousand Oaks, CA: Sage.

Pedler, M., & Burgoyne, J. (2008). Action learning. In P. Reason & H. Bradbury (Eds.), *The SAGE handbook of action research: Participative inquiry and practice* (2nd ed., pp. 319–332). London: Sage.

Prinsloo, M. (2008). Community-based participatory research, *International Journal of Market Research, 50(3)*, 339–354.

Reason, P., & Bradbury, H. (2008). *The SAGE handbook of action research: Participative inquiry and practice* (2nd ed.). London: Sage.

Rose, J. (2010). *To what extent does or can participative management work on the environment of Delta Airlines and how far and in what areas does this or will this work?* Colorado Springs, CO: Colorado Technical University.

Rossi, D. (2010). *Improving interpersonal communication and relationship-building behavior within an information technology team with emotional intelligence assessment and training.* Colorado Springs, CO: Colorado Technical University.

Sackmann, S. A., Eggenhofer-Rehart, P. M., & Firesl, M. (2009). Sustainable change: Long-term efforts toward developing a learning organization. *The Journal of Applied Behavioral Science, 45(4),* 521–549.

Sagor, R. (2000). *Guiding school improvement with action research.* Alexandria, VA: Association for Supervision and Curriculum Development.

Sapsford, R., & Jupp, V. (1996). Counting cases: Measurement and case selections. In R. Sapsford & V. Jupp (Eds.), *Data collection and analysis* (pp. 2–12). London: Sage in association with Open University.

Sawyer, R. K. (2007). *Group genius: The creative power of collaboration.* New York: Basic Books.

Schön, D. A. (1983). *The reflective practitioner: How professionals think in action.* New York: Basic Books.

Schön, D. A. (1987). *Educating the reflective practitioner: Toward a new design for teaching and learning in the professions.* San Francisco: Jossey-Bass.

Senge, P. M. (1994). *The fifth discipline fieldbook: Strategies and tools for building a learning organization.* New York: Currency, Doubleday.

Siemens, G. (Producer). (2009, 11 April). The attributes of networks. [multimedia including blogs, slides, etc.] Retrieved April 11, 2010, from http://www.elearnspace.org/Articles/connectivism.htm

Spiller, C., Erakovic, L., Henare, M., & Pio, E. (2011). Relational well-being and wealth: Maori businesses and an ethic of care. *Journal of Business Ethics, 2011*(98), 153–169.

Strauss, A., & Corbin, J. (1998). *Basics of qualitative research: Techniques and procedures for developing grounded theory* (2nd ed.). Thousand Oaks, CA: Sage.

Stringer, E. T. (1999). *Action research* (2nd ed.). Thousand Oaks, CA: Sage.

Stringer, E. T. (2007). *Action research in education.* Columbus, OH: Pearson Prentice Hall.

Swantz, M. L. (2008). Participatory action research as practice. In P. Reason & H. Bradbury (Eds.), *The SAGE handbook of action research: Participative inquiry and practice* (2nd ed., pp. 31–48). London: Sage.

Teachers College at Columbia University. (1986). Ethical issues with collaborative researchers Retrieved April 11, 2009, from http://www.otted .hawaii.edu/

Themudo, N. S. (2009). Gender and the nonprofit sector. *Nonprofit and Voluntary Sector Quarter, 38*(4), 663–683.

Thomas, R. M. (2003). *Blending qualitative and quantitative research methods in theses and dissertations.* Thousand Oaks, CA: Corwin.

Toulmin, S. (1996). Concluding methodological reflections: Elitism and democracy among sciences. In S. Toulmin & B. Gustavsen (Eds.), *Beyond theory: Changing organizations through participation* (pp. 203–226). Amsterdam: John Benjamins.

Viswanathan, M., Ammerman, A., Eng, E., Gartlehner, G., Lohr, K., Griffith, D., Whitener, L. (2004). Community-based participatory research:

Assessing the evidence. *Evidence Report/Technology Assessment, (99)*, 296. Retrieved April 11, 2010, from www.ahrq.gov/downloads/pub/evidence/pdf/cbpr/cbpr.pdf

Weick, K. E. (1969). *The social psychology of organizing.* Reading, MA: Addison-Wesley.

Weick, K. E. (1979). *The social psychology of organizing* (2nd ed.). Reading, MA: Addison-Wesley.

Weick, K. E. (1995). *Sensemaking in organizations.* Thousand Oaks, CA: Sage.

Weick, K. E. (2001). *Making sense of the organization.* Oxford, UK, Malden, MA: Blackwell Publishers.

Weick, K. E. (2009). *Making sense of the organization. Vol. 2, the impermanent organization.* Chichester, UK. Wiley.

Weick, K. E., Sutcliffe, K. M., & Obstfeld. (2005). Organizing and the process of sensemaking. *Organizational Science, 16*(4), 409–421.

Whitehead, J., & McNiff, J. (2006). *Action research: Living theory.* London: Sage.

Wicks, P. G., Reason, P., & Bradbury, H. (2008). Living inquiry: Personal, political and philosophical groundings for action research practice. In P. Reason & H. Bradbury (Eds.),

The SAGE handbook of action research: Participative inquiry and practice (2nd ed. pp. 15–30). London: Sage.

Wicks, P. G., & Reason, P. (2009). Initiating action research: Challenges and paradoxes of opening communicative space. *Action Research, 7*(3), 243–262.

Wiedow, A., & Konradt, U. (2011). Two-dimensional structure of team process improvement: Team reflection and team adaptation. *Small Group Research, 42*(1), 32–54.

Zandee, D., & Cooperrider, D. L. (2008). Appreciative worlds: Inspired Inquiry. In P. Reason & H. Bradbury (Eds.), *The SAGE handbook of action research: Participative inquiry and practice* (2nd ed., pp. 190–198). London: Sage.

Zuber-Skerritt, O. (1992). *Professional development in higher education: A theoretical framework for action research.* London: Kogan Page.

Zuber-Skerritt, O. (2011). *Action leadership: Towards a participatory paradigm.* Amsterdam: Springer International.

Index

Accountability to community, 55
Action design, 7
Action learning (AL), 11–12, 307
Action learning action research (ALAR), 12, 307
Action process log, 73–75
Action research (AR), 62
  defining, 3, 307
  examples of student work, 68–69
  history of, 3–4
  power of, 2
  process tools, 93–94
  purpose of, 49, 216
  "soft" research, 202, 233
  use of terms, 31
  See also Participatory action research
Action research (AR), perspectives on potential
    benefits and challenges
  what students say, 243–248
  what teachers say, 238–243
  what the authors say, 248–253
Action research (AR), related methodologies, 4–5
  action learning, 11–12
  action science, 4, 5–7
  appreciative inquiry, 12–13
  community-based participatory research, 9–11
  living theory, 13
  participatory action learning and action research, 14
  participatory action research, 7–9
  See also Participatory action research
Action research methodology. *See* Methodology
Action research process cycle, 3, 14–19
  AR tools, 93–94
  ethical considerations, 52–58
  networked AR activities, 190–191
  research writing and, 38, 225–229
  student proposal sample, 282–283

weekly report, 291–292
  See also Discovery; Measurable action; Reflection
Action research process cycle, practical actions
  discovery, 69–72
  examples of student work, 83–84
  measurable action, 72–75
  reflection, 76–78, 242
Action research proposal. *See* Proposal
Action science (AS), 4, 5–7, 307
Active listening, 138
Advocacy, 6
Aggregation of data, 56–57
Amalgamated Clothing and Textile Workers Union
  (ACTWU), 136
American Psychological Association (APA) ethical
  standards, 50, 51
Analysis, 209–212
  action learning's critical perspective, 11–12
  causal relationships, 110
  charting measurable actions, 207–209
  concepts of research writing, 223–224
  context, 110
  cumulative process, 209
  meaning of data, 108–109
  of personal lessons, 201
  qualitative data, 106–111
  quantitative data, 119–120
  student perspectives, 246
  student proposal sample, 284
  support resources, 131–132
  time considerations, 124
  use of reflective notes, 209
Anderson, G. L., 8, 31, 215–216, 224
Anecdotal evidence logs, 106
Appreciative inquiry (AI), 12–13, 307
Archival research, 53, 72, 131

contributions, 37
ethical considerations, 53–54
networked AR activities, 190–191
practical actions, 69–72
questions for proposal writing, 258, 267–268
reflection, 76
stakeholder needs and final report, 226–227
student proposal sample, 282
Discussion section, 260, 286
Distraction, 160
Diversity of viewpoints, 8, 55–56, 139, 146, 278
dialogic validity, 217
large groups and, 170
stakeholder inclusion, 88–89
team building considerations, 86
See also Participatory action research
Dodge, J., 100
Doom loop, 26
Dorner, Dietrich, 26–28, 135–136, 140, 158, 161
Double-loop reflection, 47, 78–79

EBSCO, 70, 222
Educative authenticity, 222
Einstein, Albert, 248
Elliott, J., 154
E-mail, 70, 72, 84, 95, 103, 131, 296
Emancipatory potential, 7, 146, 237, 239–241, 251.
    See also Personal transformation
Emancipatory research, 166, 308
Emotional intelligence (EI), 78, 81–83, 202
Ethical issues, 31
accountability to community, 55
action research process and, 52–58
addressing power dynamics, 57–58
beneficence and nonmalfeasance, 50, 55, 59, 90
business studies, 61–62
Columbia University statement, 60–61
confidentiality, 46, 53, 56, 153–154, 176–177, 197,
    302–303
continuous cycles of reflection, 58–59, 142

critical openness, 154–155
ethical codes or standards, 50–52
fidelity and responsibility, 50, 55, 59
informed consent, 46, 52, 53, 57, 301–306
integrity and transparency, 50, 55–56, 60
IRB related, 31, 37, 50, 52, 140, 150–151, 243
justice, 50, 60
network transparency, 176–177
nonprofit studies, 62
online resources, 51
participant's rights, 304–305
political correctness, 62, 63
public administration, 62
questions for proposal writing, 42, 46, 259,
    270–271
reporting problematic findings, 229–230
researcher biases, 62
respect for human rights and dignity, 51, 57, 60
risks/benefits disclosure, 50, 52, 259, 302
social networking platforms, 197
student proposal sample, 284
team approach and, 59–61
training, 52
working with people, 153–155, 158
Experiential knowing, 264, 287
Experimental research, 35, 98. *See also* Quantitative
    methods
Explicit knowledge, 201, 203, 206, 207, 233
Exploratory studies, 72, 121–122, 160
External reliability, 219

Facebook, 135
Facilitation guide for networked AR, 295–300
Facilitation skills, 90–91, 197
Facilitator roles, 185, 186–187, 295
Failure, 26–28, 135–136, 158–159, 173
reflecting on original purpose, 205–206
reporting, 201, 212, 214–215
Fairness, 222
Fidelity and responsibility, 50, 59, 309

About the Authors

E. Alana James, Ed.D., is an independent consulting professor for a number of universities. She specializes in teaching AR and basic research design to doctoral students in education, business, nonprofit management, and public administration. Her students provided the impetus for this volume. She speaks and consults internationally on the use of AR to build sustainable change in complex situations, but she also supports the use of AR for personal improvement. She is currently involved in a meta-analysis of previous AR studies. You can follow her other writing on www.ar4everything.com. Dr. James works with doctoral students to complete their dissertations, also specializing in the use of AR for thesis work, and that work can be followed on www.doctoralnet.com.

Tracesea Slater, M.S., works with Dr. James at Reinventing Life Enterprises facilitating AR and consulting with firms on the use of AR in complex situations. She recently retired from her position as the Manager of Research and Evaluation for a nonprofit in Denver, CO. Her prior research and evaluation work involved PAR projects in both education and health care for a social research company that specialized in program and organizational improvement. Tracesea's academic experience includes work as a sociology instructor at the University of Colorado at Denver and Colorado Technical University, where she leads students through the PAR process to better understand themselves and their interpersonal relationships.

Alan Bucknam, A.I.G.A., is the owner and principal of Notchcode Creative, a visual communications studio in Colorado. He has over 18 years experience in graphic design, branding, and integrated marketing. Graduating with a B.F.A. in photography from the Savannah College of Art and Design in 1993, his background includes small boutique design studios and a large private university. Since opening Notchcode in 1999, he has created award-winning campaigns for local and national clients in the nonprofit, small business, corporate, and government sectors and has been implementing the PAR process in several client branding and design products in the last 2 years. PAR lends itself particularly well to website design and development due to the medium's iterative nature and low overhead for the iterative process. He has found clients to be more engaged in the strategic parts of the design process and has seen clients focus less on their personal biases and more on the qualitative and quantitative results the process returned.

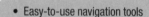